LANGUAGE AND LITERACY SERIES

Dorothy S. Strickland, FOUNDING EDITOR

Celia Genishi and Donna E. Alvermann, SERIES EDITORS

ADVISORY BOARD: Richard Allington, Kathryn Au, Bernice Cullinan, Colette Daiute, Anne Haas Dyson, Carole Edelsky, Shirley Brice Heath, Connie Juel, Susan Lytle, Timothy Shanahan

(Continued)

Playing Their Way into Literacies

Reading, Writing, and Belonging in the
Early Childhood Classroom

Karen E. Wohlwend

Foreword by
Jackie Marsh

TEACHERS
COLLEGE
PRESS

Teachers College
Columbia University
New York and London

KH

Published by Teachers College Press, 1234 Amsterdam Avenue, New York, NY 10027

Author's note: Earlier, partial versions of this research appeared as:

Wohlwend, K. E. (2008). Play as a literacy of possibilities: Expanding meanings in practices, materials, and spaces. *Language Arts, 86*(2), 127–136. Copyright © 2008 by the National Council of Teachers of English. Reprinted with permission.

Wohlwend, K. E. (2010). A is for avatar: Young children in literacy 2.0 worlds and literacy 1.0 schools. *Language Arts, 88*(2), 144–152. Copyright © 2010 by the National Council of Teachers of English. Reprinted with permission.

Wohlwend, K. E. (2007). Reading to play and playing to read: A mediated discourse analysis of early literacy apprenticeship In D. W. Rowe, R. Jimenez, D. Compton, D. K. Dickinson, Y. Kim, K. M. Leander & V. Risko (Eds.), *Fifty-sixth Yearbook of the National Reading Conference* (pp. 377–393). Nashville, TN: National Reading Conference. Reprinted with permission of the Literacy Research Association and Karen Wohlwend.

Wohlwend, K. E. (2009). Early adopters: Playing new literacies and pretending new technologies in print-centric classrooms. *Journal of Early Childhood Literacy, 9*(2), 119–143.

Wohlwend, K. E. (2009). Mediated discourse analysis: Researching children's nonverbal interactions as social practice. *Journal of Early Childhood Research, 7*(3), 228–243.

Wohlwend, K. E. (2009). Damsels in discourse: Girls consuming and producing gendered identity texts through Disney Princess play. *Reading Research Quarterly, 44*(1), 57–83. doi: 10.1598/RRQ.44.1.3. Copyright © 2009 by the International Reading Association, www.reading.org.

Library of Congress Cataloging-in-Publication Data

Wohlwend, Karen E.
    Playing their way into literacies : reading, writing, and belonging in the early childhood classroom / Karen E. Wohlwend ; foreword by Jackie Marsh.
    p. cm. — (Language and literacy series)
        Includes bibliographical references and index.
    ISBN 978-0-8077-5260-9 (pbk. : alk. paper) — ISBN 978-0-8077-5261-6 (hardcover : alk. paper)
    1. Language arts (Early childhood) — Social aspects. 2. Play. 3. Discourse analysis. I. Title.
LB1139.5.L35W64 2011
372.6'049 — dc23

                                                                        2011032128

ISBN 978-0-8077-5260-9 (paperback)
ISBN 978-0-8077-5261-6 (hardcover)

Printed on acid-free paper
Manufactured in the United States of America

18   17   16   15   14   13   12   11   8   7   6   5   4   3   2   1

9/19/10

For my family, Steve, Michael, and Greg

Contents

Foreword

There have been innumerable studies of play and literacy over the past thirty or so years, which have been richly informative about children's symbolic representations across language, literacy, and play and that have examined how play can inform children's literacy development. In this distinctive and remarkable book, Karen Wohlwend challenges us to rethink the boundaries between literacy and play, so that play itself is viewed as a literacy practice, as is reading, writing, and multimodal design; all operating as activity systems that interact to enable the production and analysis of complex and multilayered texts and practices in contemporary classrooms. This is a highly sophisticated analysis and one that is best explicated by the multi-layered and dynamic play of children in the earliest years of schooling. Drawing on a dense, ethnographic study of a kindergarten classroom, Wohlwend illustrates how, through engagement in play as a social practice, children transform the multimodal texts that they create and analyse and simultaneously transfigure their relational identities with peers in the social spaces of schooling. Along the way, Wohlwend addresses issues relating to the role of popular culture in play and literacy, constructions of gender in early childhood, and the consumption and subversion of commercialized discourses across school and peer cultures. The scope of the study, therefore, enables both breadth and depth in the analysis of the relationship between literacy, play, and multimodal design in a kindergarten classroom.

This book is important for the field in a number of ways. First, it offers new insights into the relationship between children's cultures and their social and textual practices. In the classroom in which Wohlwend acts as a careful observer, the discourses surrounding Sponge Bob and Disney princesses, amongst other media icons, become layered with the sedimented identities of individuals in the production of a range of oral, written, and filmed texts. Disentangling the intriguing, intermingled, and sometimes rather knotty threads of textual production, identity construction and the circuits of culture that circulate in the play, literacy, and design practices of children is a task that fails to daunt Wohlwend. Rather, she pulls gently at these threads, stretching them out for our greater comprehension, and teasing out their varied meanings through an analytical approach that draws on a range of theoretical and methodological approaches, such as activity theory and critical discourse analysis.

Second, Wohlwend's analysis challenges over-simplistic readings of children's play that fail to recognize the way in which children can both produce and challenge normative discourses regarding ethnicity, gender, and heterosexuality in the same play episodes. Children's social identities are formed in the intersections between family, peer, and school cultures and the social, economic, cultural, and historical discourses that circulate in any one era. Hegemonic masculinities and emphasized femininities are both appropriated and challenged by the children in Wohlwend's study and her account of this dialectic emphasizes the need to understand children's play, literacy, and multimodal design practices as being located within specific spaces and thus requiring a delicately nuanced and context-sensitive ethnographic approach. This is not to suggest that such analyses remain significant only at the local level; through her use of a variety of theoretical lenses on the construction and performance of gender, Wohlwend enables her account to speak to the experiences of educators and teachers nationally and internationally who engage regularly with the effort to comprehend the complexities of young children's identity play.

Finally, this book offers new theoretical insights into the relationship between play and literacy. Through her insistence that play *is* a literacy, Wohlwend enables us to understand the relationship between play as a mediated activity and literacy and design as facilitating symbolic representation of the world through a range of modes. As we observe young children mark-making, it is often the case that they make gestures, create sounds, and construct oral narratives that need to be seen as integral to the written text they produce and not as subsidiary to it. Further, if, as Wohlwend suggests, play is conceptualized as a form of literacy that enables the creation of a live-action text in which individual or multiple players have invested meanings, then we can begin to make sense of the multimodal, multimedia textual practices of young children as they play with Wii wands, iPads and all manner of interactive, screen-based technologies. These kinds of practices will increasingly define the play, literacy and multimodal worlds of children in the 21st century and this book helps us to trace, in much finer detail than we have previously been able to, some of the complex relationships between these various activity systems.

There is, quite simply, no going back from this book to a conceptualization of play which views it as an activity separate from or as a precursor to traditional notions of literacy. Wohlwend offers a challenge to all of those early childhood classrooms which seek to implement formal approaches to the learning and teaching of literacy and which marginalize play in the process. If play, reading, writing, and multimodal design are all overlapping and interdependent activity systems, as Wohlwend's work clearly indicates, then the continued privileging of the reading and writing of alphabetic print in schools will only serve to inhibit children's holistic development as competent and confident communicators in the digital age. This book provides a theoretical and empirical foundation for the development of new and exciting pedagogical approaches to the teaching and learning of digital literacies in the earliest years of schooling, approaches in which play is a fundamental, transformative, and tactical element; researchers, educators, and policymakers alike ignore its key messages at their peril in the decades ahead.

Jackie Marsh

Acknowledgments

Since the very beginnings of this study of playful literacies in early childhood classrooms, I have been extremely fortunate to have the opportunity to learn from wonderful language and literacy scholars. Kathryn Whitmore guided my dissertation research while demonstrating many, many practices of skillful mediation—leading, suggesting, provisioning, teaching, reading, questioning, coaching, and wise waiting. I am also deeply indebted to Cynthia Lewis, Gail Boldt, Bonnie Sunstein, Linda Fielding, Laura Graham, and Rachel Williams, for their critical perspectives, countless readings, and responsive mentoring through all stages of this book, from coursework to dissertation research to publication. Their profound influence, support, and friendship continues, in and beyond this work. I would also like to thank the University of Iowa for the UI Presidential Fellows program that supported all my doctoral coursework and research in the Language, Literacy, and Culture program.

I am very grateful for colleagues and friends who listened and responded to early imaginings and writings of this book, and encouraged me to continue: my "academic siblings" Renita Schmidt and Lori Norton-Meier and my colleagues at Indiana University: Mitzi Lewison, Gerald Campano, Carmen Medina, Donna Adomat, Ted Hall, Mary Beth Hines, Larry Mikulecky, Mary McMullen, and Kylie Peppler. My thinking has been enriched by their stimulating insights, probing questions, and connections among our overlapping research interests.

My work is inspired by and builds upon groundbreaking work by early childhood scholars working in the intersections of play, critical literacy, popular media, and classroom cultures: Anne Haas Dyson, Jackie Marsh, Vivian Vasquez, Deborah Rowe, Rebecca Kantor, Barbara Comber, and Brian Edmiston. I hope the depth of their influence is clearly evident in this book. I appreciate the careful readings and insightful editorial advice offered by series editors, Celia Genishi and Donna Alvermann, and the patient guidance of acquisitions editor, Meg Lemke, that moved this book steadily along. Thanks to the publishers and editors of the *Journal of Early Childhood Literacy*, the *Journal of Early Childhood Research*, *Language Arts*, and *Reading Research Quarterly* for allowing excerpts from earlier articles to be reproduced in this book.

My heartfelt thanks to Abbie and the children in her kindergarten—the Abbie Wannabes, the Just Guys, and the Princess Players—for welcoming me into their classroom lives so that I could learn how they play to read, write, design, and belong.

Finally, I am most thankful for the love and support of my family: to Michael and Greg, my sons and favorite teachers of play and design, and to Steve, my husband and best friend, for the encouragement and unwavering support that held our lives together through the days and months and years of this research.

Playing Their Way into Literacies

CHAPTER ONE

Play as a Literacy

November sunshine streams through the large window of the kindergarten classroom. The room is filled with light and the steadily rising chatter of children at play in small groups scattered around the room. Near the window, Lubna[1] and Mei Yu periodically check each other's work as they copy from the alphabet above the chalkboard and decorate their whiteboards with colorful letters, stars, and moons.

Amy bounces past the girls and nestles under the small wooden kitchen table in the housekeeping corner. She tucks her legs up under her chin and pulls a crocheted blanket over herself, tousled clumps of her dark blond hair poking through the yarn. She whimpers—loudly.

Colin, a tall boy with straight white-blond hair, instantly recognizes Amy as a sick child in his pretend family. He cradles the red plastic toy phone in one arm as he talks solemnly to an imaginary receptionist. "Hello, I'm calling for Amanda. (pause) Yes. (pause) Is there a check-in for that? (pause) Oh, there is? There *is*? (surprised) Well, could I just wait a while?" After a few seconds "on hold," Colin leaves a message for the doctor on voicemail. "I really don't know what's going to happen and I wanted to know if you could come over here, Dr. Barton, 'cause Amy, she has ammonia and she has the flu, and so yeah, if you could call back here—. My number is 555-3861. And my cell phone number is 555-555-888S—oops, 880, I'm sorry. Thank you."

In this book, vignettes like this one show how children at play skillfully produce texts, muster classroom resources, and perform literate identities in pretend spaces, in ways that affect their literacy learning and classroom status. Many teachers of young children will readily appreciate the early literacy in Lubna's and Mei Yu's self-imposed copying task: how they referred to the alphabet chart for models, worked to carefully form letter strokes, and drew personally meaningful texts with markers and whiteboards. What may not be as evident is how Colin's and Amy's dramatic play mattered for their developing literacy. After all, there were no pencils, papers, markers, no reading or writing of print; instead, Colin and Amy collaborated to create a storyline with credible characters in an improvised play scenario. In order to appreciate the unwritten meanings of their play actions, materials, and identities in this episode, we need new ways of thinking about texts, play, and literacy.

RETHINKING PLAY AND LITERACY

The definition of literacy is evolving to include multiple ways of interacting with, transmitting on, and navigating across screens and other media (Kress, 2003a), including films, video games, and smart phone applications. We don't just read and write printed words on a page of paper; we now blog, podcast, text message, video-record, photo-edit, and otherwise manage complex combinations of print, sound, image, and animation as we send texts across vast social networks. These digital texts are not individually authored manuscripts, rather they are multimedia co-productions shared with an interactive and collaborative audience (Knobel & Lankshear, 2007; Luke & Grieshaber, 2004; Millard, 2003).

In this redefinition, literacy is multiplied. The notion of *literacies* reflects the diverse ways we make meaning, in cooperation with others, often coordinating multifunctional tools, across networks and global sites. Moreover, the move from literacy to literacies expands the ways we think about familiar nondigital events such as play enactments, drawings, commercial toys, classroom layouts, and so on. These changes present an opportunity to rethink play as a new literacy and, at the same time, revive it as a staple of early childhood curricula. We can now recognize play as a literacy for creating and coordinating a live-action text among multiple players that invests materials with pretended meanings and slips the constraints of here-and-now realities. The embodied nature of play makes it a particularly relevant literacy at a time when the textual landscape (Carrington, 2005) is increasingly furnished with gestured texts written with Wii wands or fingers swept across screens and filmed texts captured on cell phones and uploaded to mobile screens of all kinds.

Although few early childhood classrooms provide advanced technologies that enable children to produce multimedia or engage social networks, the examples in this book show that young children can and do use play to produce and sustain collaborative and meaningful texts. (See Appendix A for a description of the methodology in the study that grounds this book, including the adapted activity model research design that coordinated ethnographic methods and three types of critical discourse analysis [Rogers, 2011].) Play allows children to draw upon their imaginations and their lived experiences and to tap into their passions and expertise. Close examination of the opening vignette shows how Colin 1) engages social practices, 2) uses available materials, 3) enacts literate identities, and 4) maintains a collaborative play space through a pretend phone call to an imaginary physician.

Literacy as Social Practice

To make this instance of pretend play startlingly real, Colin engaged in *social practices* associated with middle-class concerned parenting, healthcare consumerism, and telecommunications. We engage in social practices to carry out our individual purposes but these purposes and practices also bind us, shaped by our beliefs about who we are and what is possible or proper for us to do in a particular place (Bourdieu, 1990). The notion of a *literacy practice* (Street, 1995) recognizes that literacy functions as a social practice in a specific cultural context, that is, we use literacy to create meaningful messages but also to get things done. The purpose of Colin's phone call was to credibly enact a voicemail. He enacted the conversational ebb and flow of a phone call, followed the proper telephone conventions for leaving a voicemail message, gave the necessary medical information that a doctor might require, while using a few strategies for avoiding the waiting room of a busy clinic during flu season ("Is there a check-in for that?").

Every instance of here-and-now activity is made up of multiple social practices, and how we combine these practices matters. When particular combinations of practices come to be the expected ways of doing things, a certain combination is necessary to "pull off" (Gee, 1999) a convincing identity performance—as in the combination of calling a physician, talking to a receptionist, giving patient information, and leaving a voicemail in Colin's enactment of a medically savvy parent (Scollon & Scollon, 2004). Further, each of these social practices is made of multiple physical actions. As Colin invented dialogue on a plastic phone in the housekeeping corner, he pretended simultaneous actions necessary for placing a telephone call: handling a phone, punching in numbers, pausing for an imagined listener, repeating a phone number sequence (albeit with a missing digit), pronouncing questions with particular intonation, using appropriate conventions for politeness, and so on. These physical actions were key elements of (a simulation of) a literacy practice that creates an audio text, recorded now and accessed later via voicemail or email.

Material Resources as Modes

Colin's enacted phone conversation involved more than audio aspects of speaking on a telephone. He also made use of other *modes*, that is, the physical or sensory aspects of the material environment that are useful for making meanings. "Modes are broadly understood to be the effect of the work of culture in shaping material into resources for representation" (Kress & Jewitt, 2003, p. 1). Colin's use of modes included raising his eyebrows while repeating a question to emphasize his surprise (the mode *facial expression*), looking down at Amy briefly to assess her symptoms and then looking up while talking to a distant listener (*gaze*), quickly shaking his head and hand to indicate a mistake in his phone number (*gesture*), all while standing close enough (*proximity*) to Amy so that she could hear his conversation and the play cues for her character as sick daughter. Colin emphasized or combined these modes to best convey his intended meanings and to make his play performance more credible. Play provides plentiful opportunities for children to use modes to alter the meanings of classroom materials. For example, children in Colin's class used the physical arrangement of furniture (*layout*) in the housekeeping corner to signal "door" by knocking on air while standing in the gap between the wooden refrigerator and the sink cabinet.

Literate Identities in Discourses

The ways that Colin pulled together multiple social practices and modes marked him as a literate member, a pretend adult in this suburban community. Through play, children take up identities as literacy users in imagined communities, "communities to which they hope to belong" (Kendrick, 2005, p. 9). Every community values some practices and modes more than others, according to the dominant discourses. Discourses (Gee, 1996) are global scripts, beliefs, and power relations that influence who takes up a particular literacy identity ("independent writer," "struggling reader"), what counts as literacy, and which ways of talking, acting, and being are deemed appropriate for each identity. For example, the shaping effects of discourse are apparent in Colin's phone call. Colin followed expectations for politeness that uphold differential positioning in patient/physician identities justified by discourses in private practice medicine (e.g., addressing a physician by the formal title "Dr." but not addressing the receptionist at all, giving a patient's given name "Amanda" rather than nickname "Amy," hedging and distancing his request to make it politely indirect "I wanted to know," and requesting additional time rather than demanding immediate assistance: "Well, could I just wait a while?").

Colin's ability to successfully pull off this discourse as an appropriate "who-doing-what" (Gee, 1999, p. 23) was affected by gender, class, ethnicity, and other markers of social difference. He was able to combine literacy practices with suburban models of consumerism and parenting—practices and models that were not equally familiar to all children in the class. Like the majority of students in this classroom, Colin was White, spoke English only, and felt no need to claim a particular ethnicity or talk about his probable Euro-American heritage. Most of the 21 children (12 boys and 9 girls) lived in the surrounding affluent suburban neighborhoods. About a third of the children lived in subsidized public housing, including eight children whose families were bilingual with transnational histories in China, Sudan, Mexico, the Philippines, or Russia. It's important to remember that although play offered an important means for children to access their cultural resources, it could just as easily amplify cultural differences, exploit inequitable access, and reproduce dominant discourses.

Imagined Spaces in Classroom Cultures

Colin's phone call was constructed as "not real" because it occurred inside a play frame (Bateson, 1955/1972; Goffman, 1974), the imaginary space bounded by children's rules for pretense while situated within the everyday reality of the classroom. We can easily recognize Colin's performance on a plastic phone as an imitation of adult conversation within a play frame in the housekeeping corner. However, just because his pretense is "not real" does not mean that it is not *valid* or that is ceases to have importance outside the play frame (Bauman & Briggs, 1990). The physical actions and material objects clustered in this set of actions-and-language-with-technologies also approximate a literacy practice with technology (i.e., managing voicemail). In voicemail, a caller is expected to leave pertinent and accurate information including both land line and cell phone numbers and to correct mistakes such as an erroneous letter "S" in a cell phone number. Colin's credible playing of adult conversation allowed him not only to direct collaborative pretense in housekeeping corner play scenarios but also to confidently assume leadership roles during classroom literacy activities. He also used a pretend authority to advise other children when he played teacher during writing workshop or to assist peers in following step-by-step directions to copy a boat during a boat-building pretend learning center he invented.

Colin's example shows that young children play to navigate two classroom cultures, described in Dyson's extensive ethnographic studies of young children's composing (1989, 1993, 1997, 2003):

- *School culture* fills the official classroom space with activities, materials, and instruction provided by the teacher to support institutional curricular goals, classroom rules, and student learning.
- *Peer culture* is the child-ordered social organization of the unofficial space that operates according to "activities or routines, artifacts, values, and concerns that children produce and share in interaction with peers" (Corsaro & Eder, 1990, p. 197). Making and protecting child-governed space are among the primary concerns of

peer culture, which also include constructing a gendered identity, resisting adult culture, protecting interactive space by bonding through inclusion, and exercising power over others through exclusion (Kyratzis, 2004).

Where peer culture and school culture intersect, as often happened in this kindergarten, a potentially transformative space is formed where teachers and children can mediate school and perhaps expand opportunities to participate (Fernie, Kantor, & Madrid, in press).

SITUATING PLAY IN CLASSROOM CULTURES

School Culture and a Playful Kindergarten Classroom

The play-based approach to literacy in this kindergarten was unique within this school. Play was not often the focus of classroom activity in the school at large—or even in other kindergartens just down the hallway. In this school (and in other schools where I observed and taught[2]), there was an overwhelming emphasis on skills mastery (e.g., letter sounds, word recognition) that left little room for traditional play periods in kindergarten. In the last decade, U.S. newspaper articles (Brandon, 2002; Hemphill, 2006; Stewart, 2005; Weil, 2007) have regularly reported moves to replace playtime in kindergarten with "more academics," often in the form of increased literacy skills practice through worksheets, workbooks, flashcards, and computerized drills. School district policies, federal grants, and state standards drive teacher accountability programs aimed at raising student achievement, measured through standardized tests. Faced with high-stakes testing in which low student scores result in school closings and job loss, many teachers and administrators opt for the most defensible approach and focus on discrete skills instruction that closely matches test content (Ravitch, 2010; Stipek, 2006). Where literacy is equated with discrete skill tasks, play is often characterized as nice but too trivial for the serious business of schooling, an expendable frill with little potential for improving literacy achievement. Preschools and kindergartens, no longer safe havens from the pressures of teaching to the test, focus on teacher-directed instruction and practice (Adler, 2008; Brandon, 2002; Daniel, 2007; Magee, 2003; Stewart, 2005; Stipek, 2005).

However, the central argument of this book—the recognition of literate value and cultural power in play—challenges this widespread trend toward scripted instruction and constricted literacy in early childhood education. The examples in the following chapters show that children used play to access literate identities as readers, writers, and designers, allowing them to become more proficient and critical text-users of print, image, and action.

Importantly, their play also multiplied pathways into school literacy: All the children in the class met the district's end-of-year literacy benchmarks for kindergarten.[3]

The kindergarten featured here was unusual, providing a rich case that illustrates this reconceptualization of play as an embodied literacy. The classroom was located in a public elementary school that primarily serves families in suburban neighborhoods in a Midwestern university community. The kindergarten teacher, Abbie Howard, was an experienced teacher with a learner-centered inquiry-based approach to preschool and kindergarten teaching that drew upon children's interests and cultural resources; the following vignette provides a glimpse of a typical day in this playful kindergarten.

> The morning begins with Settling In. Children enter the classroom to the soothing strains of Yanni or Enya, or other instrumental slow-paced music that plays softly in the background. As children arrive, they check the Morning Jobs chart. These routine tasks involve "signing" various charts by moving tokens, wooden popsicle sticks, or clothespins labeled with children's names. Children sign up for lunch by placing their name tokens in miniature hot or cold lunch pails, choose a literacy center by clipping a clothespin on the chart, or read the question of the day and respond by clipping a clothespin on the yes or no column. After signing in, children fan out across the room as they take out puppets, flannelboard sets, puzzles, taped books, writing folders, and journals.
>
> "I have something to tell you, so listen carefully." Lilting snippets of invented song like this float around the room all through the morning, as Abbie catches children's attention for a minute and then relinquishes it just as quickly so that they can resume their projects. From the moment the children enter the classroom, they continually select from a range of choices to map out a unique learning path for themselves each day. Abbie, a tall woman with short brown hair, sympathetic eyes, and a calming voice, pauses occasionally in her rounds, kneeling to listen seriously to excited discoveries about hornworm caterpillars or bitter disputes over the ownership of a prized pencil.
>
> After all the children arrive—about 15 minutes or so—Abbie invites the children to gather in the center of the room with a sing-song welcome that she improvises on the spot. Abbie assembles the group into the Family Circle whole-class meeting area for sharing and planning time.

Next, she explains her planned activities and adjusts the day's agenda displayed on a large pocket chart to include the activities that children suggest. Once the plan for the day is settled, Abbie perches on the edge of an oversized oak rocker for shared reading of poems, songs, and a featured big book on the adjacent story easel.

Fifteen minutes of outdoor recess provides a break between shared reading and the rest of the morning. Kindergartners have three recess periods on the playground each day: 15 minutes at midmorning and midafternoon, and 25 minutes at lunch. When the class returns to the classroom, Abbie briefly introduces Literacy Centers, a 30-minute period of adult-supported activity at the reading table, art table, writing table, listening center (books and tapes), and the Family Circle area (big books, story easel, song and poem charts, and classroom library). During Literacy Centers, children work on literacy and inquiry activities in four small groups led by an adult, either a teaching paraprofessional, a visiting pre-service teacher, a parent volunteer, or Abbie. An additional group usually works independently in the Family Circle in the center of the room: reading picture books or big books, retelling flannelboard stories, playing audiotapes as they read song charts, or listening to taped books at the listening station.

After Literacy Centers, the class regroups on the ' circle rug in front of the rocker for a second Family Circle meeting. Abbie recaps discoveries from different groups and a few children share work samples as they transition into Writers' Workshop. Abbie reads a picture book and connects the book to a writing mini-lesson and demonstration at the easel. She usually invites one or two children to participate in a quick shared writing, encouraging comments and connections by everyone. "Put your finger on your chin if you know what you want to write about." Abbie asks the children individually about their plans for Writers' Workshop as they trickle off to work on projects collected in their writing folders or stories in their journals. During Writers' Workshop, Abbie circulates and conferences with children individually or in small groups. Author's Chair provides a chance for two or three more children to share their writing as children gather once more in Family Circle.

Abbie next introduces activities for Choice Time, the final period of the morning. Choice Time includes most of Literacy Center areas and others as well: blocks, math, snacks, housekeeping corner, and the dollhouse. Abbie circulates during this center period as well, teaching as she facilitates children's activities. Literacy Center and Choice Time activities usually blend literacy, play, and design through inquiry explorations such as staining and washing fabric, weaving, and paper-making. Although the school district has implemented a basal series for language arts instruction, Abbie selectively chooses from the commercial curriculum to allow more learner-directed activity and to make time for Writers' Workshop, Literacy Centers, and play periods. She worries whether policies at the national, district, or school level will continue to allow her the freedom to integrate the inquiry activities that she feels are vital to an engaging curriculum.

The official and unofficial spaces in this kindergarten classroom privileged different literacies, materials, and modes. The school culture valued reading and writing with print, evident through the prominence of literacy in teachers' classroom schedules and curriculum standards set by the community school district and federal educational policy (NCLB, 2002; Schmidt, 2005). Reading and writing practices with books were the focus of almost all of Abbie's planned curricular activity during the mornings. In peer culture, play practices with toys and dolls and design practices with paper, markers, and tape were highly valued by children.

- Play: Practices included *enacting* performances in the housekeeping corner, *animating* toys in the dollhouse, or *exploring* tools and materials at the art table.
- Reading: Practices included *approximated reading* of print and image in familiar books, big books, and charts in the Family Circle classroom meeting area.
- Design: Practices included *drawing* images and *constructing* artifacts at the art table.
- Writing: Practices included *approximated writing* of print and *authoring books* with print and speech at the writing table.

Figure 1.1 shows relationships between school and peer culture, places in the classroom, and the four kinds of literacies: play, reading, design, and writing[4]. Each literacy operates as its own activity system through supporting materials: reading through the district balanced reading curriculum, writing

Figure 1.1. Overlapping Literacies and Classroom Cultures

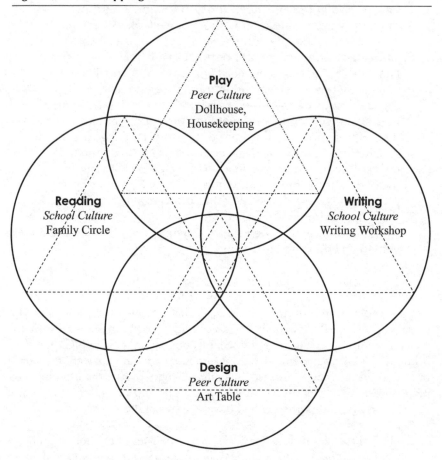

through the kindergarten version of a writing workshop, play through children's popular media, and design through several boys' shared interest in competitive sports. In the diagram, the triangles within circles represent literacy activity systems within the peer and school cultures at various locations in the classroom (discussed in the next chapter).

Peer Culture and Three Play Groups

Children participated in socially organizing classroom worlds by forming friendships and play groups in peer culture. Play groups were fluid, with children joining and leaving throughout the morning as they followed their interests. However, three groups were more stable and became affinity groups (Fernie, Kantor, & Whaley, 1995) as children chose to play together regularly based on their common interests and shared play themes. Within these groups, children helped each other learn to read, to draw, and to write as they played together[5]:

> *Abbie Wannabes* enacted the role of teacher as they read and played school together.
>
> *Just Guys* explored materials and design tools, in their words, by "just playin' around" as they drew pictures and constructed paper toys about the local university football games.
>
> *Princess Players* animated small dolls as they acted out stories and authored books about Cinderella, Snow White, Sleeping Beauty, and other Disney Princess heroines.

The three play groups were situated in a shared social history of children's friendships in the classroom. The sociogram in Figure 1.2 maps social relationships among play groups and the intersections of peer and school cultures. In the figure, arrow patterns indicate children's relationships according to their *reported* play companions. A child's placement within a play group (ovals on the figure) indicates that child's *observed* involvement with that group's shared practices and play themes. For example, Garrett is placed near but not in Just Guys. Although he indicated several of the children in the Just Guys group as preferred playmates, my observations showed that he often chose to read alone or to draw about animals from *Madagascar* rather than sit with other Just Guys to draw about sports, *SpongeBob SquarePants*, or *Star Wars* themes. Further, children like Garrett who are placed on the periphery of the sociogram were less popular than those in the center. On the other hand, children like Emma or Zoe who easily bridged groups are placed in the center (inside dashed line circle). These children had a wider range of play opportunities, were chosen more often as preferred playmates, and were more likely to change activities frequently and move across play groups.

THEORIZING PLAY AS A LITERACY

Children learn to read, write, and design by collaborating with others who help them to interpret and represent meanings in a specific cultural context, in this case, a kindergarten classroom. Scollon's (2001b) notion of *nexus of practice*—a community's intricate web of insider practices, expectations, and dispositions—explains how play operates as a literacy for making meaning and participating within peer and school cultures. Nexus theory draws upon two powerful constructs: *mediation* in cultural historical activity theory (Leont'ev, 1977; Vygotsky, 1935/1978) and *habitus* in practice theory (Bourdieu, 1977).

Figure 1.2. Sociogram: Relationships between Three Play Groups and Children's Preferred Playmates

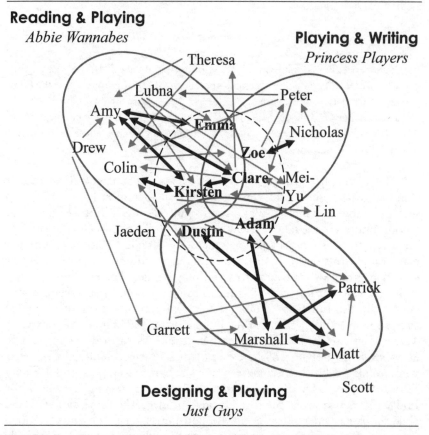

Reading & Playing
Abbie Wannabes

Playing & Writing
Princess Players

Designing & Playing
Just Guys

Note: Gray one-way arrows point to a child's preferred playmates. Black two-way arrows indicate children who mutually selected each other as preferred playmates. Children were asked to name three children that they usually play with at Choice Time. Children with no outgoing arrows indicated "by myself" or "with anyone," and those with no incoming arrows were not selected by another child.

Mediation and Literacy Practices

Mediation involves physical manipulation of objects: turning the pages of a book, moving a pencil to make marks on a paper, or handing a folded paper to someone. Clusters of these physical actions become literacy practices (Street, 1995) when they are categorized as social practices (e.g., book-handling, copying a word, giving a friend a birthday card) that communicate meanings and carry out mediating functions (e.g., sharing ideas, influencing others, and participating in the sociocultural environment) (Scollon, 2001b; Wertsch, del Rio, & Alvarez, 1995). Literacy develops as children take up more and more complex literacy practices, sometimes facilitated by peers or teachers (Rowe, 2008, 2010). In this way, a kindergarten operates as a *community of practice*, an apprenticeship into literacy and schooling in which learning is marked by an increasing participation in core practices that allows learners to take up a progression of identities from newcomer to expert (Lave & Wenger, 1991). Through play, children can mediate print texts for themselves (Vygotsky, 1935/1978) and others by pretending to be more experienced readers who use more complex literacy practices, allowing them to play the expert within the classroom community.

Mediation is multidirectional so that every aspect (e.g., beginning readers, teachers, books, pencils, hand and eye movements, strategies, and so on) of a literacy practice is simultaneously mediating and mediated (Engeström, 1987; Leont'ev, 1977). Texts are mediated by literacy practices in ways that make their meanings accessible; for example, we make sense of a printed page in a book through the literacy practice of reading. When literacy practices are used to mediate the world, the practices in turn are mediated as new ways of reading and writing emerge. For many of us, the practice of reading now involves scrolling and sweeping a finger across a touchscreen and we ourselves are mediated when new literacy practices become our accustomed ways of thinking and making sense of the world (e.g., "Is there an app for that?"). Play has unique facility for mediating collaborative texts as well as classroom identities and social relationships.

Habitus and Nexus of Practice

Literacy practices—and expectations for when, where, how, why, and by whom they should be used—are learned through participation in families, schools, and communities during early childhood, gradually becoming engrained and absorbed as familiar embodied and automatic patterns of daily life. We engage in everyday activities without noticing the ways in which our actions signal *habitus*, the histories of practices and dispositions shared among a group of people (Bourdieu, 1977). Nexus of practice refers to this network of backgrounded, valued practices. Nexus of practice marks membership when the combinations we expect—the things we "just know" how to do (e.g., passing someone on a sidewalk, making eye contact, a slight nod, "How are you?") elicit automatic reactions from others that signal co-recognition (e.g., an appropriately brief response "How are you?" rather than a longer response that misinterprets this perfunctory greeting as a request for information).

In communities of practice, key nexuses are explicitly demonstrated to novices to help them learn how to perform—and to want to perform—valued practices. For example, kindergartners are taught particular ways of handling books or behaving while reading or writing (e.g., printing neatly, sitting up straight, working quietly) that have little to do with literacy (Luke, 1992) but that serve as automatic, embodied markers of a *good student* identity. Moreover, the desire to be recognized as a good student produces further practices and aspirations that uphold school hierarchies and relational identities (Holland, Lachicotte, Skinner, & Cain, 1998) such as teacher/student or proficient reader/struggling reader within the field of schooling.

Modes and Sign-making

Play, like other literacies, produces *signs*, material objects or actions that represent and communicate ideas (Kress, 1997; Siegel, 2006; Wohlwend, 2008). Children make signs by resourcefully and flexibly using whatever "comes to hand" and seems apt for the purpose (Kress, 2003b), that is, children are designers who strategically emphasize modes, the best-fitting sensory aspects of materials, to represent the crucial parts of the meanings they want to convey. At the same time, these purposive, economical representations can be temporary and fluid, shifting in meaning from moment to moment. In play, the symbolic meaning of a discarded cardboard box fluidly can shift from container to chair to dollhouse to stepping stool within the space of several minutes. "The real point about this voracious appetite for semiotic recycling is the child's ever-searching eye, guided by a precise sense of design, both for material and for shape" (Kress, 1997, p. 104). These design decisions are shaped by children's interest or the social purposes they want to accomplish.

Interest involves more than a child's intended meaning or a social goal (Rowsell & Pahl, 2007); it also reflects the knowledges, identities, social practices, and dispositions learned at home and school. In other words, children's products reflect their nexus of practice. Kate Pahl found that making a bird from tissue paper layered one child's knowledge of chickens on his family's farm in rural Turkey, a pet name that his mother had for him, a teacher's reading of *The Ugly Duckling*, and a prior bird-making craft activity at school. This handmade artifact was as much a product of these histories as the immediate design practices and modes used to craft it. In this way, children's drawings and other design products are layered with *sedimented identities* deposited through a child's choices of materials and modes, practices valued by families, schools, or communities, and identities situated in prevailing discourses (Gee, 1999). "The text, then, becomes an artifact of identities as much informed by social practice, habitus (Bourdieu, 1977), and context as it is by the material choices made during its creation" (Rowsell & Pahl, 2007, p. 392).

Discourses and Identities

Children's play links to overlapping global discourses about children's agency, creative expression, developmentally appropriate teaching, and school accountability that sanction the dominant ways of doing school in kindergarten. For example, the play ethos (Smith, 1988) is a widespread and romanticized early childhood educational discourse that characterizes play as agentic and all good for all children (Roskos & Christie, 2001). However, play can just as easily constrain children by reinforcing existing social identities and power relations in classroom cultures.

A particular identity often resonates with other complementary or contradictory identities in other discourses, enabling a dynamic, multifaceted representation of self with meanings that may be imposed, unintended, or strategic so that in this kindergarten classroom, different identities were available to a child drawing pictures at the writing table, to a child playing with telephones in the housekeeping corner, and to a child animating a princess doll in a pink and lavender dollhouse.

OVERVIEW OF THE BOOK

My goal in this book is to reconceptualize play as a literacy; this reconceptualization is also a tactic that holds promise for convincing administrators and policymakers to make room for play in schools. Many advocates for play in early childhood education have depended upon the play ethos and its widely held assumption that children *need* play as part of a developmentally appropriate educational program (Roskos & Christie, 2001). The more expansive definition of literacy outlined in this book re-centers play in school curriculum as a valuable semiotic system in its own right and revalues play as an essential element in "new basics" (Dyson, 2006) that aim to prepare diverse learners to respond to rapid change in the 21st century.

Each of the three main chapters in the book examines play from one aspect of nexus of practice (i.e., practices, materials, or discourses). The chapters show how the messiness of play opens opportunities for accessing, mediating, and improvising texts with available resources within the constraints of school. Each chapter provides in-depth interpretation of meaning-making among one play group of children in a featured literacy play nexus: Chapter 2 analyzes the playing/reading nexus, Chapter 3 the playing/designing nexus, and Chapter 4 the playing/writing nexus. Classroom examples illustrate how the transformative power of play intensifies when merged with other literacies. The final chapter looks across nexuses to see how Abbie and the children used play as a space-making tactic that manipulated school power relations by producing alternative contexts and importing otherwise unavailable identities and discourses. Finally, a set of appendices provide methodological explanations and key examples for each critical discourse analysis approach.

Chapter 2 details how children learn to read as they play school. Using mediated discourse analysis (Scollon, 2001a), I examine play as an action-oriented literacy in a kindergarten that operates as a literacy apprenticeship. By combining reading and play practices, Abbie Wannabes created a nexus that strengthened peer mediation and allowed them to teach each other and try out new strategies while pretending to be expert readers. Although an apprenticeship tends to reproduce existing power relations, the playing/reading nexus expanded what counted as reading and who could be recognized as readers, reconfigured children's social status in this classroom, and proliferated ways for children to "do school."

Chapter 3 shows how children competed and taught each other as they produced drawings and artifacts. Using multimodal analysis (Kress & Jewitt, 2003; Jewitt, 2006; Norris, 2004), I examine how a group of boys used the playing/designing nexus to produce sports logos, football drawings, SpongeBob puppets, and other art projects to pull off identities as talented designers. During the creation of these artifacts, Just Guys strategically appropriated available modes and materials for meaning-making. Their design practices sedimented into the artifacts they created so that a child-made paper airplane served as a toy, as evidence of design expertise, and as a badge of membership among group members who competed to be recognized as the best designer. In this way, artifacts represented the child designer's intended meaning through the choice of materials but also produced cultural capital that helped them cordon off a boys-only social space for enacting dominant masculinities.

Chapter 4 shows how children's doll play, authoring, and playwriting revised gendered identity texts in children's popular media. Using critical discourse analysis (Gee, 1999) consistent with activity theory (Lewis, Enciso, & Moje, 2007), I uncover the discourses layered into media toys and child-made artifacts along with meanings, materials, and design practices. The Princess Players, a group of boys and girls, used the playing/writing nexus to appropriate and rewrite popular culture identity texts by twisting and remixing Disney Princess storylines as they animated dolls and toys in the dollhouse and authored books, puppet shows, and plays. Children's attempts to faithfully replay the familiar Cinderella and Sleeping Beauty roles conflicted with their desire to take up more empowered positions as self-rescuing princesses or as authors and directors. In the face of these tensions, the transformative power of play produced improvisations and escapes from confining hyper-feminine princess identity texts with requisite happily-ever-after endings.

In Chapter 5, I draw upon de Certeau's (1984) distinction between strategies and tactics to explain the tensions that children faced during play at school. As in other institutional places, strategies upheld school goals while tactics allowed individuals to "make do" and create space for their own purposes. For example, Abbie's pedagogy was a tactic that fused (Millard, 2003) four literacies—playing, reading, writing, and design—producing an inclusive space where children could play with meanings *and* achieve school goals as they enacted literate identities in both peer and school cultures. Conceptualizing play as a tactic also acknowledges its unique facility for allowing diverse learners to try on more empowered identities, allowing them to experience—and perhaps invent ways out of—the constraints of dominant discourses in school. These play transformations produce critiques and escapes, open access to cultural resources, and reconfigure classroom power relations, making play a promising critical literacy in early childhood classrooms (Comber, 2003).

CHAPTER 2

Playing School and Learning to Read

The day begins as Abbie settles into the big oak rocker that anchors Family Circle, the kindergarten meeting place on the round fuzzy rug in the center of the classroom. The children at the front of the group snuggle close to listen to *The Keeping Quilt* by Patricia Polacco. Emma, her upturned face framed by long tangles of blond hair, listens intently while sucking her thumb and fingering the pastel pink fleece of her sweatshirt sleeve. When Abbie closes the book, Emma leans forward and points to the scalloped gold medallion on the cover, "I love that story. It won a reward. A flower reward!"

ABBIE WANNABES, NURTURE, AND FAMILY CIRCLE

Family Circle, the name for the class meeting area in Abbie Howard's kindergarten, blurred the line between home and school, capturing the nurturing atmosphere that permeated this early childhood classroom. To ease children's transition from home to school, Abbie worked to make the physical environment as familiar and comfortable as possible. Floor lamps, rocking chairs, and oversized pillows softened the school-issued bright plastic and laminate furniture. Soothing music accompanied every activity period so that occasionally a few lulling notes of Enya would waft through the clamor of children at play.

In daily sessions in the Family Circle meeting space, Abbie transformed the class into an imagined school family in which she enacted the role of nurturing parent and children were expected to care about and be kind to one another. In Family Circle, Abbie gathered the children together for read-alouds and shared reading, often choosing books with themes of acceptance and tolerance for others. As she read, Abbie invited children to read along, comment, and make connections—in other words, to actively participate in making meaning with books with her support (Holdaway, 1979). In these shared reading experiences, students participated by predicting, identifying known words, tracking print, and chiming in on repetitive phrases as Abbie read oversized "big books" and charts. Whenever she read aloud, Abbie frequently paused to comment or wonder about the illustrations or to make connections to other books or class experiences. These modeled comprehension strategies sparked excited responses from the children. In some kindergartens, children might be scolded for "blurting out" spontaneous comments; instead, Abbie solicited, expected, and respected these reader responses. She especially valued children's comments that connected the book to their life experiences or to other previously read books. As in Emma's example, many children not only offered comments but also their own unsolicited evaluations, comments regarding illustrations, phrases, or the entire book, ranging from "I love that story" to "Yuck."

During playtimes, children relived these shared reading experiences by sitting in the big rocker and pretending to be Abbie as they reread familiar big books to each other. Strong attachment to Abbie was evident in children's enactments as they copied her actions, voice, songs, and phrasing. One group of teacher players, Abbie Wannabes (four girls—Emma, Lubna, Amy, Kirsten, and two boys—Drew and Colin, who was introduced in Chapter 1), regularly pretended to be the teacher as they played school and read books in Family Circle area. Like Abbie, children in this play group were primarily White monolingual English speakers, except for Lubna whose family self-identified as African internationals. Lubna's grandparents and extended family still lived in Sudan and she was bilingual in Arabic and English with developing literacy in both languages. The other Abbie Wannabes—Emma, Amy, Kirsten, Drew, and Colin—did not self-identify ethnically and their shared European-American blondness is naturalized in the Midwestern United States as commonplace and unremarkable. When I first observed Abbie Wannabes playing teacher, I wondered if they were simply reproducing and enforcing the classed, raced, and gendered power relations of schooling by taking up the role of "little teacher." However, closer examination revealed that their play involved complicated negotiations that shifted the meanings of texts and their classroom identities.

This chapter illustrates nexus of practice in Abbie's kindergarten through a model of an early literacy apprenticeship, showing how Abbie Wannabes transformed the meanings of the texts they read as well as their classroom identities. Following an overview of the range of Abbie Wannabes' typical play and reading practices, two excerpts from this group's play illustrate the *playing/reading nexus* where Abbie Wannabes merged teacher play with their early reading practices. In the playing/reading nexus, reading strengthened play and made a pretend teacher's performance more credible—*reading to play*—evident in an example when Emma read a book while playing teacher to draw in an uncooperative peer. In addition, such pretend play in the playing/reading nexus strengthened their reading abilities—*playing to read*—when children who played teacher taught reading strategies to other children. These instances also reveal how teacher play can reproduce disparate literate identities and classroom status, complicating assumptions that play and mediation operate as benevolent processes. Mediated discourse analysis of moments of negotiation in one particularly transformative playing/reading event reveals how Lubna's playful teaching helped Adam, a more accomplished reader, make sense of the print and images in a book, and how both children accessed literate identities as readers, teachers, and learners. These examples from the playing/reading nexus reveal the complexity of play negotiations and situate peer mediation in overlapping discourses of schooling—overlaps that can reproduce but also disrupt classroom power relations.

PLAY, READING, AND LITERACY APPRENTICESHIP

Colin stands next to the wooden cupboard in the imaginary grocery store in the housekeeping corner, reading the nutrition label on an empty carton of orange juice. "Hmm. Vitamin D." He sniffs the opened spout. "Eeeew. It sort of smells like orange juice." Taking the red plastic toy phone off a cupboard shelf, he tells Scott, "Let's pretend this is a speaker." Colin picks up the receiver and talks into the mouthpiece, "88, please call line 1." Scott suggests, "There's a fire," and Colin immediately takes up the emergency theme. "We have a fire in here! I have to call 911." At first, Colin continues to use the phone more like a loudspeaker—he doesn't dial but speaks immediately into the phone, making an announcement rather than an emergency call—"Firefighter, we have a announcement here. There's a fire in our store." Emma adds, "We're locked in." Scott offers a strategy for escaping the fire, "I have the key in my pocket." Emma quickly responds, "Only *you* can get out." Colin is holding the receiver but begins flipping through the phonebook. He suddenly recognizes a name, "John??" Play is suspended as all three players inspect the name of a classmate in the phonebook. Emma is the first to revive the scenario by announcing the arrival of the firefighters, "They're here!" Colin calls on the phone again; this time he dials 911 before saying, "There's a fire in here. We need more help."

Playing Together, Making Meaning

In the malleable world of pretend play, children learn to work together to make, negotiate, and sustain *shared meanings*—interpretations of events or texts that are discussed and collaboratively accepted—as they talk and enact scenes. Play creates a child-governed space to sort through and explore the meanings of everyday activities such as the purposes and uses of loud-speaker announcements, emergency calls, and phonebooks. Colin, Emma, and Scott's play activity in the housekeeping center involved *enacting*: The children coordinated their pretend adult roles as they blended sociodramatic play themes of grocery shopping and firefighting.

The children's exploration of the shared meanings associated with a grocery store emergency produced a play frame (Bateson, 1955/1972). A play frame is a framework that shifts a physical reality into a pretend situation that then must be actively maintained through player negotiation (Goffman, 1974). When two or more children collaborate in play, they often find that they must stop to clarify shared meanings to keep the play scenario going. Children orchestrate play enactments when they step back and talk to clarify roles, propose new character actions, or redirect storylines. Abbie Wannabes frequently revised their play narratives as they adjusted and co-ordinated their shared meanings. The need to clearly define the rules for the play frame created breaks where children stopped playing and negotiated their character roles to agree upon next steps or the meanings of their props before returning to pretense. Vygotsky (1935/1978) theorized that such flexible manipulation of meanings in dramatic play "leads directly to written language" (p. 111) as children flexibly separate conventional meanings from objects and then attach new meanings to create play props. In this way, the manipulation of meaning and symbols during play resembles reading and writing processes that manipulate graphic signs to symbolize meanings.

Shared meanings are coordinated through a range of directives outside and inside the play frame, apparent in the children's enactment of the grocery store emergency:

- explicit propositions or directives that openly refer to pretense (Auwarter, 1986; Trawick-Smith, 1998): "Let's pretend this is a speaker" explicitly alerts players that they must use the phone as a microphone (and implicitly directs them to listen as Colin makes an announcement over a pretend public address system).
- implicit propositions or directives spoken "in-character" within the flow of play such as through dialogues between characters (Göncü, 1993; Sawyer, 1997): Scott speaks as one of the characters to propose an escape: "I have the key in my pocket."

- explicit propositions or directives spoken in a "director's voice" when addressing another actor: Emma's "Only you can get out" alters Scott's proposed escape; her restriction prolongs the play scenario by limiting the number of players who can escape.
- self-directives that manage the actor's own character (Martin & Dombey, 2002; Sawyer, 2003): "I have to call 911" makes Colin's intention clear, to others and to himself.

Sociodramatic play, or enacting adult roles in imaginary work settings (e.g., house, restaurant, hospital), allows children to create their own contexts for exploring cultural practices and to make sense of these practices through their shared meaning-making (Göncü, 1999; Owocki, 1995, 1999). At the housekeeping center, children regularly used play to import everyday scenes from their homes and neighborhoods. Family scenes such as cooking meals in the kitchen were most common, but children also pretended a variety of familiar community sites and literacy practices: writing prescriptions and medicating "kitties" in a vet clinic, taking orders and preparing desserts in a Dairy Queen, and reading labels and purchasing food at a grocery store. Further, these dramatizations were not bounded by the housekeeping center; children also pretended as they laundered fabric at the art table, dug imaginary weeds in the soil at the sensory table, or as in the next play excerpt, read picture books to an imaginary class in Family Circle.

Playing Teacher, Doing School

Drew sits on the edge of the oversized wooden rocking chair and leans over to read the agenda for the day, pointing to each word in the familiar sentences printed neatly on paper strips tucked into the blue nylon pocket chart. He adds teacher comments periodically, pitching his voice very high and sing-songy to imitate Abbie's practice of improvised musical messages, "At Choice Time, get some hand gel." When he reaches the end of the last sentence, he picks up a glitter-filled transparent plastic pointer to read through the poetry sentence strips on another pocket chart.

As Drew read the charts, he tapped each word, moving in a left-to-right direction across the chart, pausing at the end of each line, glancing at several children seated on the carpet in front of him, and calling on just those children who raised their hands, the accepted practice for signaling the desire for a turn to speak. Drew's enactment of teacher demonstrated that he knew how to engage and combine the expected, almost automatic give-and-take between teachers and students that make up the usual ways of doing things at school. By playing the teacher, he temporarily claimed the central position of expert in this classroom community of practice[1] a more empowered role than his position as novice student.

In communities of practice, the normally tacit ways of doing things are foregrounded for novices so that they can easily acquire them (Scollon & Scollon, 2004). In the introduction to schooling, classroom routines and expected student dispositions are exaggerated and explicitly introduced to kindergartners. In some kindergartens, learning to "do school" is a high priority and routines are practiced until young children can automatically perform the nuances of institutional practices: for example, walking down a hallway, silently in a group, single-file with hands at their sides, a practice unique to schools, prisons, and military processions. As children learn the foregrounded routines modeled for them, they also learned the background-ed ways of talking, handling materials, and positioning selves and others that are necessary to "pulling off" a good student identity at school. In contrast, in Abbie's classroom, everyday routines were open to negotiation; the daily agenda could easily be altered to accommodate children's ideas and her foregrounding of school-valued practices emphasized mediation over institutional standardization and compliance.

Abbie's mediation layered on another kind of apprenticeship, scaffolding children into a community of developing readers and writers. This kindergarten operated as an *early literacy apprenticeship* where children were invited into literacy through mediated encounters with print. For example, Abbie modeled reading strategies to make them apparent and accessible: She paused in her reading, waiting for children to chime in and gradually handing off the responsibility for reading to the children (Holdaway, 1979; Rogoff, 1995; Wells, 1986). When Abbie Wannabes played teacher, they mimicked the early reading practices that Abbie had modeled during shared reading. For example, as Drew read the daily agenda, he touched and matched each word on the sentence strips to phrases that he had memorized.

Reading by Approximating Text

Readers negotiate a tension between following the conventions of print on the page (e.g., matching letter sounds to graphic symbols, tracking left to right, word recognition) and inventing a personally and culturally sensible meaning for the text (e.g., predicting from lived experiences, drawing upon a storehouse of cultural meanings) (Whitmore & Goodman, 1995). When approximating print to read, children drew upon personally meaningful contexts, memorized bits of familiar books, and emerging knowledge about alphabetic print. Knowing a story "by heart" allowed children to match memorized phrases to illustrations, words, or lines of print on the page.

Children approximated print to read familiar texts on sign-up charts, poems, song charts, pocket charts, class schedules, daily messages, and the oversized big books that Abbie read to the class during shared reading sessions. As they read, children often shared strategies with each other as they worked to coordinate their inventive sense-making with their knowledge about conventions of print. It was not uncommon to see children head-to-head puzzling over a word that didn't come out right as they attempted a one-to-one matching of spoken words to the written words on a page. Children invented sensible stories to match book illustrations, tracked print with plastic pointers to sing and read along with an audiotape, framed words for closer inspection with fly swatters adapted for that purpose, retold a familiar book on a flannelboard with felt story sets or on story aprons using small stuffed character dolls, and read their own written books with personally memorable spelling patterns.

Inventing stories from illustrations

> Amy is playing teacher, sitting in the rocking chair with the picture book *Have You Seen Birds?* flopped open across her lap. Lightly touching each illustration, she moves through the book rhythmically, "Duck, Duck, Goose," pausing after each page to turn the book outward so that her imagined audience can see the pictures. When she reaches the end page, Amy snaps the book shut and announces, "Singing time! Singing time!" She scrambles down off the rocker and darts across the room to get a song chart.

Abbie Wannabes chose books from the array of library books on the large wooden bookshelf and perched on the oak rocker as they invented to read picture books to an imaginary audience. As Amy invented words in response to the clumps of birds pictured on the page, she applied the rhythm of a read-aloud and attached a meaningful context to the pictured content. She recited "Duck, Duck, Goose," appropriating the words from a popular chasing game. Through the practice of inventing stories, children combined their knowledge of story-reading performance and book-handling practices with the meanings that they inferred from pictures and genres in trade books, big books, signs, lists, charts, and other classroom texts.

Reading along with an audio-recorded song

> Emma and Kirsten stand over the hand-lettered song chart that lies across the reading table. With headphones snugly hugging their ears, they tap through the lines of the

song with glitter pointers, skipping across the words on the
song chart and singing slightly off-key, karaoke-style. Kirsten
picks up a jeweler's loupe from the science table to magnify
and examine the text, enlarging the print as she slides it
along the line of print. Emma begins copying the song's title,
"It's a Beautiful Day" (by Greg & Steve, *We All Live Together*,
Vol. 4) on a Post-it note, explaining, "We haven't sang it
in a while." She writes a note to "Mrs. Howard" asking
Abbie to sing the song in the next Family Circle meeting.
Emma finishes copying the title and takes the Post-it over to
Abbie's desk where she attaches it to the edge of the desk
next to the computer.

Children independently reread familiar books and songs with the support
of audiotaped recordings at two classroom listening centers, in electronically
enabled shared reading experiences. One of the areas was a listening station
with a tape recorder, a jack with four headsets, and four copies of a picture
book that had been read previously during Family Circle. However, this
center was seldom chosen by the children. In contrast, someone could almost
always be found tapping out music in the song chart area; favorite songs
included "Sing" by the Carpenters and Louis Armstrong's rendition of "It's a
Wonderful World." To read a song chart and sing along with the CD player,
children needed to adjust the speed of left-to-right tracking and timing of the
return sweeps according to the pace of the song. Children sometimes stopped
the tape and framed words for closer inspection, locating familiar words to
find their place in the song or to compare words across song charts.

Framing words

Amy sits in the wooden rocker holding up a song
chart entitled "Peace." She directs Emma to "find *you*."
As Emma scrutinizes each line of the 20+ lines on the
chart, Amy repeats, "Find *you*," adding helpfully, "Y-O-U."
Emma replies, "I'm trying to find it! There's no *you* on it."
Amy lays the chart on the floor and searches until she is
satisfied that the word is not in the song. Unperturbed,
Amy regroups, "Find *e*," and Emma immediately points
out *e* after *e* on the chart.

Children in the classroom located single words, particularly classmates'
names, and played invented word-framing games. At times, children framed
words to display skill in recognizing known words. At other times, children
framed words to decode unknown words in order to match an envelope to

a friend's mailbox or to read an empty "SpaghettiOs" can before dumping its imaginary contents into a bowl to feed the baby doll.

Retelling with props

> Colin spreads out a blue story apron on the Family Circle rug and arranges a brightly colored assortment of stuffed felt characters next to it. Laying the book on the carpet, he kneels over the text to read *The Napping House* by Don and Audrey Wood. Colin takes the fly swatter from Lin, who is framing words by placing the cut-out opening in the plastic mesh over words on the page. Lin, who could read independently in English and Chinese, was swiftly sliding the fly swatter from word to word. Admonishing her not to "put things on the book" (his invented rule), Colin reverses the fly swatter and uses the handle to point out words on the pages of the open book. As he reads each page, he carefully velcroes another stuffed character to the nap of the story apron. Colin uses remembered phrases to read the familiar text but stops suddenly, "A wakeful flea? Oh no, that can't be right." He reads the phrase again, "A wakeful flea who bits . . ." Lin quietly corrects him, "bites" and Colin places the flea at the top of the velcroed stack of felt dolls on the story apron.

Children used an assortment of props—puppets, flannelboard, story apron dolls, favorite toys from home—for retelling stories, both with or without accompanying books. In this example, Colin drew upon his memory of the book to attend carefully to the text and approximate the printed words as he narrated his placement of the felt dolls on the story apron. When Abbie Wannabes used puppets to enact a picture book in the classroom library, they explored new perspectives as they took on character identities in play and extended their understanding of literature. Play enriches language in retellings through improvisation, character perspectives, and talk that organizes roles, clarifies shared meanings, and keeps play going (Göncü, 1993; Pellegrini & Galda, 1993; Rowe, 1998, 2000; Sawyer, 1997, 2003). Young children express deeper understandings of books when they dramatize the stories through play. "[Dramatic play] allows children to walk around in story settings. It allows them to touch, feel, and actually look at objects from the vantage points of book characters" (Rowe, 2000, p. 20).

Rereading own writing

> Lubna reads the journal page that she has just written to the other children at the table, tracing a finger under the

letters "IMLRNEGHIWot skpt." "I'm learning how to skate."
She pointed to the p-ish-looking letter in the middle of her
approximation for *skate*, "I messed up on the 'a'." In contrast
to Lubna's dark skin and tightly plaited thick glossy black
braid, her self-portrait shows a white girl with a spray of
long yellow hair.

Reading from self-invented forms presented a set of affordances and
challenges different than approximating conventional print. On one hand,
children knew what they intended to write and if they recalled the context
from an accompanying illustration or read their messages shortly after
composing, they could easily attach meaning to their written print. On the
other hand, the practice of reading back over the text often caused children
to notice when their printed letters didn't match a remembered message and
they would stop reading, sometimes to revise or edit their writing. When
Lubna noticed that she "messed up on the 'a'," she picked up a marker and
added a long curl to the bottom of the letter, apparently to make it more
a-like. Interestingly, Lubna made no changes to her picture. Her color choices
could have been unintentional or intentional: Children often used whatever
marker was "to hand" (Kress, 1997) to color their drawings; however, it
is also possible that Lubna intended a portrayal of self that matched her
teacher's and friends' race and ethnicity.

In addition to informally reading what they had written to others sitting
nearby, there were several structured opportunities each morning for children to read their writing to the entire class. During Family Circle sessions
before and after Writers' Workshop, Abbie's rocking chair was transformed
into the Author's Chair in which children shared their written work and
designs. Each day, several children took turns sitting in the Author's Chair
to read a journal page or child-made book and then ask for comments from
the audience, calling on two or three children who raised their hands for a
turn. Children in the audience usually responded to the author with a short
general affirmation, "I liked it" or "Good reading." From Abbie's perspective, the purpose of Author's Chair readings was to celebrate children's writings and to point out interesting features that other children might explore
in their own writing. From the children's perspective, the social act of calling on friends for comments seemed more important than listening to the
content of peer responses. Author's Chair allowed children to call on a few
chosen friends and to demonstrate friendship; whether someone was called
on or not was the source of momentary triumph or sudden disappointment.
The social value of this chance to recognize and be recognized as friends
was apparent when Dustin declined to call on anyone to respond to one of
his readings. Patrick immediately protested and called out for "Comments!
Comments!" in an effort to reinstate the response period and the opportunity to be recognized by his friend. Lubna's and Patrick's responses show

that rereadings provided numerous opportunities to affiliate with others, to be recognized as someone who belongs.

THE PLAYING/READING NEXUS

When children combined playing and reading practices, they created moments dense with ways to read, to do school, and to belong. The combination of reading and play illustrates one nexus or set of intersecting valued practices in this classroom's nexus of practice. Figure 2.1 maps the social space where practices of approximating text and enacting were integrated by the Abbie Wannabes play group. The playing/reading nexus (starred point) is the space where play and reading practices interact. This nexus is situated in a third space (Gutiérrez, Rymes, & Larson, 1995) created by overlapping school and peer cultures: Reading is a prime concern of the official school space while play is a staple of unofficial space of peer culture. The placement of the Abbie Wannabes group (white dotted oval in Figure 2.1) reflects both their integration

Figure 2.1. Abbie Wannabes in Playing/Reading Nexus

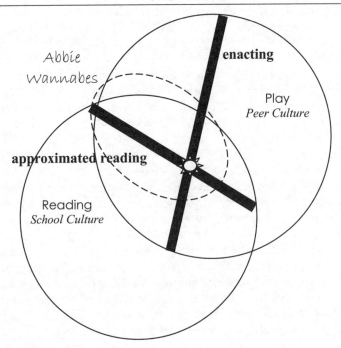

of reading and play practices and their teacher play that actively bridges school and peer cultures. The next section examines two transformative events in the playing/reading nexus as Abbie Wannabes approximated text to read as they played school.

Reading to Play

> In a quiet corner of the kindergarten classroom, Emma perches on a wooden chair, reading. As Emma pages through a nonfiction picture book on trees, she confidently invents a sentence for each illustration. She holds the book off to one side and reads "It can be every kind of tree in the whole wide world" for a picture depicting several varieties of trees.
>
> "Hey, Emma!" Peter's shout interrupts her solitary reading. His call is an implicit challenge and a playful invitation to engage in a tussle over classroom rights; he wants her to notice he is sitting in the child-sized rocker across the room in Family Circle. Sitting in the rocker is an honor reserved for the "Helper of the Day," the child appointed to carry out coveted classroom chores. Affronted, Emma marches over immediately to reclaim possession of her space, "Hey, *I'm* the helper of the day!"
>
> Grinning, Peter scrunches his sturdy frame deeper into the squeaky leather cushion. He won't budge. After giving several ineffectual commands to "get outa there," Emma improvises. She walks to the teacher's story easel and resumes reading invented passages but in a noticeably louder voice. When her volume attracts the teacher's attention, Emma points to Peter and explains, "I'm pretending he's the helper of the day and I'm the teacher." As Emma reads, she adds teacherly asides to Peter. Finally, she directs him to "Get right here," tapping and pointing with her sneakered foot to indicate the space on the carpet where Peter should sit. Obediently, he leaves the rocker and sits cross-legged at her feet as she continues to read.

Emma shows how reading a book while playing the teacher transformed a classroom meeting area into a pretend school space where children could assume identities as readers and leaders. As Emma read while playing school, she appropriated a familiar literacy practice and classroom materials to authenticate her teacher performance and to maneuver an uncooperative peer. In the following sections, I draw from this vignette to illustrate how

Figure 2.2. Kindergarten as Apprenticeship in an Activity Model

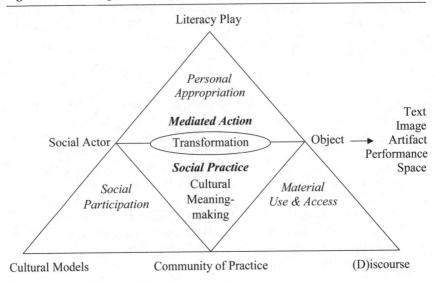

an adapted activity model explains the early literacy apprenticeship that structures Abbie's kindergarten. The model incorporates several dimensions suggested by Scollon's (2001b) notion of a nexus of practice. In Figure 2.2, the four triangles within the larger triangle represent four planes that shape literacy and play nexus: cultural meaning-making, personal appropriation, material use and access, and social participation. I use the four planes to interpret Emma and Peter's playing/reading activity, showing how this nexus of play and literacy practices allows social actors to 1) attach cultural meanings by 2) individually appropriating and transforming physical actions and materials into practices and artifacts according to discursive expectations and shared histories of 3) uses for materials and tools and access and 4) social participation within a community of practice.

Cultural meaning-making

Cultural meaning-making is a process that turns physical actions into meaningful social practice, always interpreted according to a specific cultural context. For example, reading and play practices consist of multiple *mediated actions* (Wertsch, 1991), physical actions that use literacies to alter the meanings of objects. As Emma pretended to read the print in a picture book, she carried out simultaneous mediated actions: handling a book, turning pages, tracking print, looking over illustrations, inventing phrases to fit illustrations, and so on. In some classroom cultures, the interpretation of this set of actions is "immature pre-reading" or "playing around." However in literacy apprenticeships, the mediated actions clustered in this set of actions-and-language-with-a-book constitute a valid reading practice for making sense with a text through inventions that approximate conventional forms (Whitmore, Goodman, Martens, & Owocki, 2004). Emma's invented phrases (e.g., "It can be every kind of tree in the whole wide world") and actions (holding a book to show the pictures, tapping to a place to sit with her foot) are neither wild guesses nor mere imitations but represent sense-making transactions with text (Goodman, 1994; Rosenblatt, 1978) and strategic improvisations (Bourdieu, 1990; Holland, Lachicotte, Skinner, & Cain, 1998) that moved an obstinate peer but within the constraints of classroom rules that prohibited physically dragging him from the chair.

Personal appropriation

Personal appropriation describes the agentic and strategic use of available materials for the child's own purposes (Kress, 1997; Rogoff, 1995). Early literacy researchers (Dyson, 1997; 2003; Kendrick, 2005; Rowe, 2008, 2010) demonstrate that young children are not passively encultured into schooling through unidirectional top-down apprenticeship but that they use literacy play to enact identities and to produce social spaces that blend school and peer cultures. Children appropriate "textual toys" to cross social boundaries in school culture (Dyson, 2003) or to play adult literacy users. As Emma pitched her voice across the room, she appropriated a book and a teacher role to strategically position an uncooperative classmate.

Social participation

Social participation is a process of belonging within a community by engaging in its valued practices. In a literacy apprenticeship, increased participation signals learning so that children's competence with literacy practices directly links to their social identities and status within the classroom (Christian & Bloome, 2004). To be accepted as a credible performance, literacy practices must not only incorporate conventional forms valued in the classroom but must also be accompanied by other expected, albeit backgrounded, practices. Emma's foregrounded reading practices were accompanied by backgrounded practices of playing the teacher and following school rules. As Emma read and tapped with her shoe to indicate a spot on the floor, she copied the way teachers control errant students through backgrounded nonverbal directives that run concurrently within the foregrounded spoken lesson. When valued practices like these link and strengthen each other, their combination comes to be expected and their intertwined performance serves as a marker of membership and insider knowledge (Scollon, 2001b). These nexuses animate discourse (Gee, 1996), a community's set of shared tacitly held beliefs that signal membership and shape what counts as appropriate. Emma's foregrounded reading practice, accompanied by play enactments of backgrounded ways of doing school, signaled her competence as a student as well as her status as a lead player.

Material use and access

Our use and access to materials are constrained by an object's embedded histories that invoke expectations for its proper uses and appropriate users. Books, toys, and tools are tangible texts with durable, portable, discourse-laden meanings (Brandt & Clinton, 2002). Books activate implicit expectations for right-side-up orientation and front-to-back page-turning by ideal readers (assuming English language conventions). As a child acquires the desire and practices to read a book, the book acquires the child by invoking its embedded "theories of a task" and "theories of a person" (Scollon, 2001b, p. 124). In Emma's book, the contrast of large colorful illustrations beside nondescript black print supported her inventing from the pictures rather than the words. Her picture reading appropriated the "unintended affordances" in literacy materials that prompt pivots to playful, unexpected uses not always envisioned by teachers (Bomer, 2003, p. 231), including the use of books to manipulate others.

The following instance from another example of Emma's teacher play in the playing/reading nexus illustrates that even apparently well-intentioned mediation produces ideological effects, as in the following interaction between Emma and Jaeden, the only African American child in this primarily White class.

Playing to Read

"This one is awesome!" Jaeden exclaims as Emma and he page through a rack of song charts. Each teacher-made song chart has a popular song lettered onto poster-sized cardstock, taped to a plastic clotheshanger so that the children can hang them up on a metal rack.

Emma picks out one of her favorites, "It's a Beautiful Day," and the two children get to work arranging the necessary materials on a nearby table: Emma places the song chart flat on the tabletop and puts on a pair of headphones attached to a tape player. Jaeden brings two glitter sticks from the story easel. As she looks for the accompanying tape, Emma knocks over a small vase of daisies on the tabletop. A passing parent volunteer tells the children to get a paper towel to wipe up the water that is pooling along one edge of the table and trickling onto the floor. Neither child moves. Jaeden points out to Emma, "It's getting on the floor!" Emma replies, "It'll dry," but leaves the table to get a paper towel.

As Emma wipes up the spill, Jaeden inserts a tape into the tape player but cannot locate the play button to start the song. He asks for Emma's help and she insists that he wait to start the tape recorder until she finishes wiping up the spill.

Jaeden protests, "I'm just in kindergarten. I'm not like the other people. . . . You don't like me."

"I do like you. I just have to dry the table first."

With the spill dried, Emma straightens the song chart for "The Number Rock" (by Greg & Steve, *We All Live Together*, Vol. 2) on the writing table.

Meanwhile, Jaeden jokes by talking into one of the headphone earpieces, "Hey, can you hear me?"

Finally, the song is playing and both children are tapping pointers along the chart. After a few minutes, the children remove their headphones and invent a word-finding game in which Jaeden is to find and frame the words that Emma spells for him, "Do you see T-W-O?"

He touches *two* and Emma responds with praise and more words to find, "Yeah! You found it! One, one, one, Wo—oo!" She immediately spells another word for Jaeden to find, "S-i-x."

When Jaeden cannot find *six*, Emma repeatedly spells "s-i-x", and also gives more specific clues to the word's location on the chart, "Somewhere on the third row." She taps two words with her glitter pointer to narrow the field, "It's one of these two."

Jaeden, points to the word, "I did it! I'm the winner!"

Next, Jaeden and Emma search for new song charts and Jaeden chooses "It's a Beautiful Day" and Emma picks out "Kids Are Beautiful People" (1997, Judith Brown and Mel Wheeler). She adjusts the headphones on her head and once the music starts, she taps out the words to this unfamiliar song. Jaeden lays the song chart on the table and listens, tapping out the beat on his hand with the glitter stick. The song ends and Jaeden announces, "My turn. Put mine in."

Emma writes a note to Abbie on a Post-it to request that the class sing "Kids Are Beautiful People" at the next Family Circle meeting. Jaeden tries to switch tapes and asks Emma for help with the buttons, "Emma, I don't know how to do this." She points to the play button. Jaeden presses the button to start the tape but then wraps the headphone cord around his waist. He calls out loudly, "I'm stuck." Abbie comes over to help him and Emma explains, "I'm helping Jaeden get going." When Jaeden tells Abbie that he figured out how to operate the buttons on the tape player, Emma objects, "I showed him every time."

Emma's word hunt allowed Jaeden to practice matching spoken words to print, to look closely at visual features of a word, and to demonstrate word-framing skill. Jaeden "won" the game by correctly pointing to a word that Emma selected for him. The children's invented game is consistent with prevalent school literacy practices in which children responses are evaluated for how well students follow directions (Bloome, Puro, & Theodorou, 1989) or display skills (Cazden, 1988; Mehan, 1979) rather than how well they make meaning with a text. Such interaction patterns emphasize teacher power by tightly controlling student responses. Abbie Wannabes aligned themselves with the teacher through their play and used reading, nurturing, and teaching as a way of taking charge. It's telling that their pretend teaching activities centered on shared reading (teacher as primary actor and speaker, usually standing or sitting above the others, directing children's attention to an object she holds) rather than shared writing (child as primary actor, teacher as questioner, usually sitting next to child at eye level, looking at words or pictures as the child writes). The object of Emma and Jaeden's game was as much about following the play teacher's directions as it was about Jaeden's reading, perhaps more.

Educational discourses circulate visions of learning and schooling with ideals for good teachers and good students. Discourses shape and are shaped by classroom nexuses of practice that students eventually internalize and embody in their individual bodily habitus. Marjorie Siegel and colleagues (Siegel, Kontovourki, Schmier, & Enriquez, 2008) describe the nexus of practice necessary to be recognized as a successful literacy learner in the discourse of balanced literacy during reading workshop:

> children were expected to sit on their assigned carpet square, hold their bodies in a "perfect magic 5" (described on a wall chart as "legs in a pretzel, hands in your lap, mouths closed, eyes forward, ears ready to listen") and speak only when called on by the teacher. But when they moved to independent work time, the expectations for participation shifted, and students were to engage in any

number of practices with their assigned "partner," such as sitting back to back and reading separate books, taking turns reading books to each other, and stopping to talk about books with their partners. (p. 92).

Allan Luke (1992) theorizes that teacher control of students' bodies, posture, and physical actions with pencils and books practices in early literacy training inscribes discourses with student identities and power relations into their habitus.

> (1) . . . the discourses of pedagogy are built around claims about "truth" and the "real" which in turn are transformed and rearticulated in the multiplicity of material practices deployed in the site of the classroom. There (2) a disciplinary inscription of the subjectivity of the student occurs, contributing to the construction of a bodily habitus (Luke, 1992, p. 115)

Discourses of schooling legitimate teacher/student power relations. The nurturing discourse so prominent in Abbie's teaching constructs children as innocents who need teachers. To take up positions as nurturers, we position ourselves as responsive to children's needs, thereby foregrounding their *need* for us. Early childhood teachers (typically women) are constructed as facilitators who suggest rather than direct, who protect, care for, and comfort rather than punish (Grumet, 1988). In this vignette, Emma was positioned as teacher and as competent player and reader: She wiped up the spill, she operated the tape player, she spelled the words, and she directed Jaeden. In contrast, Jaeden embodied the role of needy child, waiting for more competent others to take care of the spill or to start the tape recorder. For the most part, he was content to let Emma do these things for him. However, this dependence had a price: When he did learn how to start the tape cassette on his own, Emma took the credit and undermined his claim that he had learned to do this himself, saying, "I showed him every time." Jaeden did not experience Emma's teaching as scaffolded mentorship. His comments, "I'm not like other people" and "you don't like me," indicate that he felt rejected and excluded, rather than nurtured. Jaeden was not a regular member in this or any other play group; he usually joined groups briefly and then moved on to another activity. Children who play alone are often individuated and constructed as lacking social skills when, in fact, exclusionary practices and shared social histories of the entire group should be addressed (Wohlwend, 2004). His positioning as the only African American child in the class implicates race in this distancing from other children. At least, his comments signal that his classroom experience was not one of unproblematic and scaffolded progression to the center of a community of practice but rather frustrating encounters with raced and gendered discourses of schooling.

AUTHORITY AND MEDIATION IN THE PLAYING/READING NEXUS

Play clearly mediates identity just as reading mediates texts. Mediation involves transforming an identity or an author's idea into a personally meaningful form according to one's personal history and repertoire of social and cultural contexts. Pretending to be Abbie often required children to transform into imagined readers, who in turn transformed texts to make the print meaningful. As pretend teachers, they taught each other new strategies for operating electronic reading aids such as tape recorders as well as strategies for interpreting texts, analyzing pictures, and handling books. Play is neither trivial nor innocent; Emma's teacher play shows that the playing/reading nexus intensifies identity-building activity by combining two transformative literacies in way that reproduced inequitable power relations between nurturing adult and needy child, teacher and student, and European-American and African American identities.

However, playing/reading nexuses also held potential to disrupt social stratifications and reconstruct power relations, as illustrated in the next vignette. This sketch describes an 11-minute instance of playful peer mediation in which Lubna's teacher enactment directed the group and supported her own inventive picture reading of a small primer, *The Three Little Pigs* (Parkes & Smith, 1987). At the same time, she mediated another child's word-by-word reading of the book's text as the group collaborated to enact the story using a flannelboard set of felt characters. This event is a particularly rich example of pretend play as the children engage in a "play within a play," two levels of pretense as they pretend to be the flannelboard characters as they play school.

> In the center of Family Circle, Lubna, Adam, and
> Colin sit around a flannelboard, a poster-sized cardboard
> rectangle covered in black flannel. Lubna, playing teacher,
> is reading aloud, making up words to match the pictures in
> a paperback reader, *The Three Little Pigs*. Three pink felt pigs
> are arranged on a large red felt house on the flannelboard.
> Lubna flips to the final page of the book and reads,
> stretching out words for dramatic effect, "And huffed and
> blo:::wed[2] the house down. They hided in the—no:::o."
> Lubna jerks the book up, out of Colin's reach, as he
> leans over to attempt to turn the page, "Do you have to
> turn—"
> "No." Lubna looks back at the book and directs Adam
> to put the felt wolf on the flannelboard, "It's your turn
> now."

As she reads, "They found a big pot, SPLI:::SH," Adam flies the wolf off the flannelboard in howling spirals.

Attracted by the wolf's howls and Lubna's expressive storytelling, Amy leaves the wooden rocker and sits down at the edge of the flannelboard. Lubna reads, "And the wolf went away," and leans over to tap the corner of the flannelboard. Adam places the wolf near the spot that she indicated and drags the wolf away from the scene across the nubby tan carpet. Leaning back, Lubna reads, "And they lived happily ever after" and closes the book.

Immediately and without negotiation, Lubna sets up the flannelboard to start the story over again. She removes the red house and the pigs and places the mother pig felt cut-out on the flannelboard. Adam returns, twirling the wolf around a finger.

Lubna hands the book to Colin, "Your turn to read." Obediently, Colin opens the book.

"What do you want to be?" Lubna turns to Adam, who is now twirling the wolf above his head.

Amy proposes an innovation on the story that adds another character to be played by the pink felt mother pig. "The four little pigs."

Adam turns to Colin, "I want to read the book." Lubna ignores Amy and asks Adam, "Do you want to read the book? Okay, you read the book." In a simultaneous motion, she takes the opened book out of Colin's hands and hands it to Adam while taking the wolf piece from Adam and handing it to Colin, saying, "I thought you didn't *want* to read the book. What happened to you guys??" Smiling at this joke, she sits on her knees, leans back and signals Adam to begin reading. "The mom—no!"

Lubna objects as Colin removes the yellow felt straw house from the flannelboard. Lubna swiftly replaces it and turns to Amy, pointing her finger, "And you're the last pig." She straightens the three pig characters next to the mother pig.

Lubna cues Adam to begin. He holds the book in front of his face and begins to read softly but the others don't hear him over the buzz of classroom activity. Lubna peeks over the top of his book and offers advice from time to time, "When I don't know a word . . . I just say something" and "Don't look . . . make it up," dividing her attention between

Adam and her other pretend students. (Lubna's mediation of Adam's reading is detailed in Table B.1 in the Appendix B.)

Finally, Adam hands the book back to Lubna and she reads the rest of the story, holding the open book out in one hand and reading the pictures loudly and expressively.

"The big bad wolf." Lubna stops, looking around for the wolf felt piece, and reaches a hand out to Adam, who is now walking the wolf along the carpet. "'And he puffed—'"

Amy reaches to take the first pig off the straw house, "I was the first one."

The play stops as Lubna stops reading to clarify roles. Pointing to each player, Lubna explains, "No, Amy. I was the first, and then Colin, and then you. And then you could be the mother. I was going to read this [page] and Adam has that [wolf piece], and Adam is after you."

Amy insists, "I was in the first house."

Changing tactics, Lubna explains, "But we came after you. That is over."

Lubna resumes reading the book, "And he huffed and he puffed and he blo::wed the house down."

As the story continues, Drew and Jaeden come to sit on the edge of the flannelboard to watch. Peter bounds in and swoops down, waving two Powerpuff Girls dolls, "Ow-ooo-Ow!" Annoyed at Peter's interruption, Colin frowns at him.

Lubna places the book on the floor and finishes, "He ran a::ll the way home." Peter scoots next to her on the carpet with a Powerpuff Girl in each hand and announces "I'm Bubbles." Lubna objects to this feminine superhero role and corrects him, "No, you're the Professor."

Responding to Peter's interruption of the Three Little Pigs, Amy tells him, "Don't play with us."

Lubna turns back to her sharply, and says, "Don't say that. He's my friend!"

"Yeah, but he's not s'posed to have those [Powerpuff] girls wif us."

Lubna replies, "He likes those. All right, let's clean this up."

In this instance, the physical layout of children seated around flannelboard materials reinforced power relations among their play identities, affecting who controlled the text and, ultimately, which text versions were authorized. Lubna's place at the flannelboard authorized her view as the official view and positioned her as teacher (Gee, 1999). Lubna's place determined the baseline so that the other children viewed the story action on the flannelboard from sideways or upside-down perspectives. As Lubna distributed materials, she also distributed their associated roles and practices: books for narrators to read, or felt pieces for actors to animate. As teacher, Lubna held the power to manage role negotiations for the story, to start and stop the text, to control moves in and out of the inner play frame (the animation of felt pieces as characters in a folktale), and to lead the talk outside the play frame about shared meanings. The children gave little attention to maintaining the outer play frame, that is, the enactment of teacher and school. Teacher play was so much a part of their play group activity that almost no effort was needed to maintain play identity relationships between pretend teacher and her pretend students. This unspoken recognition provides further evidence that their play interactions made up a nexus of practice.

The children also tacitly accepted the differential positioning that came with playing a teacher or student. Each teacher-player in this scenario had regularly played the teacher and knew the expectations for both roles; obeying the teacher's directives without objection was customary and almost automatic. Lubna, the pretend teacher, not only dictated who could handle the materials throughout the play sequence but also which elements of the text could be altered. When Amy proposed a departure from the book's storyline with the addition of a fourth little pig, Lubna ignored Amy's proposition and preserved the book's cast of characters. However, she later gave Adam considerable freedom when she urged him to improvise and "just say something." This pattern of proposition-rejection-reversal is not unusual in children's play negotiations. Young children take the content of their play seriously as imaginary scenarios are built through heavy expenditures of ideas and social capital (Corsaro, 2003). Children invest deeply into play frames, pouring in time, talk, and friendship bonds to develop a collective plan. These social costs determine who is allowed to join a group, driving exclusionary tactics as young children attempt to protect the fragile play frames that they co-construct (Corsaro & Eder, 1990). When play practices linked and integrated with readings of text, children's protection of a co-constructed play frame was complicated by a need to protect their individual or collective interpretations of the story text. The negotiation of a tension between improvisational play and conventional reading of text shaped more than play scenarios and text meanings; it also shaped children's identities and social relationships. For example, Lubna's efforts to preserve the authority of the text and to keep the play going strengthened her own authority as the pretend teacher as children looked to her for help. Because Adam was concerned with matching a spoken word to print in a familiar but difficult book, his reading stalled while Lubna, who invented readily and referred to the pictures more than the print, moved through the text quickly and confidently. Lubna's inventive reading and play-based me-diation supported Adam's near-conventional reading as he stopped to frame a word and she responded by looking at the illustration, inventing phrases, and offering advice to prompt him to move forward. (See Appendix B for an explanation of mediated discourse analysis of the playing/reading nexus, including close mediated discourse analysis of 2 minutes from this episode of peer mediation between Lubna and Adam.)

Integration of reading and play practices reinforced classroom values for cooperation, inclusion, and peer mediation. As Lubna enacted the teach-er and directed and read the story, she attended to classroom values for co-operation and inclusion while strictly enforcing her version of the text through her direction of the other children. The authority of the text over the children's play is evident as Lubna, as the pretend teacher, dictated what was and was not possible in the story. Other players also protected their shared meaning and co-constructed play space: Amy objected to Peter's introduction of Powerpuff Girls into their heavily negotiated and now-established interpretation of *The Three Little Pigs*, even though she herself had repeatedly proposed a departure from the text with the addition of a fourth little pig.

William Corsaro (2003) suggests that young children engage in exclusion-ary tactics to protect their fragile play frames. The playing/reading nexus adds another layer and intensifies this protective tendency, complicated by a need to protect their interpretation of the authorized story text. In the children's enact-ment of *The Three Little Pigs*, tensions in the reading event (between a reader's creative meaning-making and an author's textual authority) layered onto ten-sions in the school pretense (between player agency and [pretend] student obe-dience), shaping children's activity in complex and contradictory ways. For ex-ample, after 10 minutes of directing other children and tightly controlling the play scenario, Lubna reacted to Amy's play-protective but exclusionary tactic by admonishing her and affirming Peter as a friend who has a right to bring Powerpuff Girls into the flannelboard play by explaining, "He likes those."

Play identities influenced who could control the text and which text ver-sions would be authorized. Amy's attempts at transforming the text to allow her to use the mother pig character as a fourth little pig were unsuccessful, in part because she proposed the change from a less empowered play iden-tity of student and was unable to overturn Lubna's refusals to accept impro-vised additions to the cast. Lubna as teacher also held the power to start and stop the text and to control moves in and out of the inner play frame (the flannelboard animation of *The Three Little Pigs*) that allowed her to close explicit play communication about the role negotiations.

Negotiating Authority through Peer Mediation

Play expectations for teacher/student roles reversed classroom identities and allowed Lubna, an expressive and inventive player/reader who made up stories based on the pictures, to coach Adam, a nearly independent reader who was beginning to read simple chapter books (e.g., the Henry and Mudge series by Cynthia Rylant). Lubna offered a shared reading teaching strategy: She said the first part of the sentence and trailed off to let him fill in the rest. The sentence she said, "And the mama says . . ." did not match the sentence printed on the page: *Once upon a time, there were three little pigs.* Instead, it was an invented version that corresponded to the expected dialogue for the first character on the flannelboard. Lubna's directive, "You're supposed to read it," caused Adam to look closer at the text and then to show Lubna the print. The story playing stalled as Adam focused on accurate decoding of a single word. Lubna then offered to help Adam read the text. It's important to note that her focus was on Adam rather than the text: "I'll help you read it" instead of "I'll read it." It was a teacher-like offer to share responsibility in order to read a tricky part rather than a move to take over his role as narrator. Interestingly, Lubna's strategies for helping Adam to read aligned with my informal analysis of his reading. When Adam read this book to me, he often stopped reading when he came to unknown words or asked for my assistance rather than checking illustrations or using story context. My own recommendation as an early literacy teacher would echo Lubna's advice to invent and keep going through the tricky spots to help keep the meaning of the story intact.

Mediating School Identities

In Abbie's classroom, Lubna could participate as a central player and social leader in the learning community. This is not always the case for transnational children whose social standing in the classroom and opportunities to develop linguistic competency are often diminished by restrictive language policies (Christian & Bloome, 2004). In kindergarten classrooms where literacy equates with mastery of alphabetic forms, Lubna's inventive and expressive reading could be overlooked, devalued, and even discouraged. Abbie's expanded view of literacy as a mix of storytelling and sense-making recognized Lubna's play performances of reading as valid and meaningful.

It's worth noting that by the end of the school year, Lubna and the rest of children in Abbie's classroom read very well by any kindergarten standard. As in typical kindergarten classrooms, children learned to identify letters, to sequence story events, to match language sounds to symbols, to read holistically remembered books, and to read small amounts of connected text in unfamiliar books with familiar words and strong picture-text match. Additionally, children in Abbie's classroom read purposefully, connected what they read to lived experiences at home and in the community, pored over books and songs and puzzled out meanings with friends, and expressed personal aesthetic responses to literature. In this early literacy apprenticeship, children learned to access, interpret, and transform literacy as a way to gain status in print-valued school culture.

MEDIATION AND DISCOURSES OF SCHOOLING

As the Abbie Wannabes read and played *The Three Little Pigs*, they taught each other valued reading practices that enabled them to independently produce further literacy events but also to circulate a discourse that promoted children's agency. Agentic discourse manifested in peer mediation and child-directed learning as children typically consulted and assisted each other before seeking out Abbie or other adults. Peer mediation enabled personal appropriation as children strategically took up materials for their own purposes and cultural meaning-making as children pooled their cultural and linguistic resources to co-construct meaning. Lubna's previous experiences as a novice within scaffolded literacy sessions supported her peer teaching, enabling her to appropriate Abbie's modeled practices; Lubna's appropriation allowed her to mediate Adam's approximation of the text. In Family Circle sessions, Abbie's foregrounded reading practices were accompanied by backgrounded teaching strategies and Abbie Wannabes emphasized these backgrounded practices for teaching through play identities as pretend teachers and through classroom identities as helpful peers.

Peer mediation produced transformative cultural meaning-making in this small excerpt from one instance of literacy play. Children transformed a book into story and play, changing print and image into action with props. By appropriating the pictured storyline and rephrasing print into dialogue for pieces of felt, children transformed themselves into fictional characters in their flannelboard play, into teachers and students in their school pre-tense, and into readers in the classroom. Their interactions with the book transacted the tension between readers' interpretation and authors' intended meanings. They grappled with the boundaries of text: How much of the text could be changed? What words should be used? Which characters should be allowed? Adam, the reader, worked at an exact reproduction of the print on the page, focusing on reading the words and figuring out the conventional forms but losing the meaning and the players in the process. Lubna, the player and storymaker, worked at faithfully representing the meaning of the traditional folktale, making up words to keep the flow of the story but allowing no change to the cast of characters or plot. Together, they helped one other to attend to cultural conventions to interpret the book's meaning and symbols, to coordinate the whole with its parts.

Abbie Wannabes also used books to enforce compliance and to limit each other's access to materials, empowered by an accountability discourse of standardization that promotes teacher authority and expectations for ac-curacy and conformity. Expectations for a single correct text interpretation are made concrete in the material features and historical uses of a school primer (Luke, Carrington, & Kaptitzke, 2003). Although Lubna could in-

vent phrases, she still worked to preserve the storyline; her personal appropriation was bounded by adherence to the traditional meaning of a folktale
and her strong sense of story. Abbie Wannabes also activated "pervasive
cultural models of reading" outside their immediate kindergarten experience: through "sounding out" (Compton-Lilly, 2005, p. 441) and teacher
enactments that emphasized teacher authority and child compliance in ini-
tiation-response-evaluation turn-taking (Cazden, 1988; Mehan, 1979) and
an insistence on hand-raising.

An infinite number of constitutive relationships could be drawn between
a classroom, its materials, and particular discourses (e.g., the discourse of
teacher agency in Abbie's pristine teacher's manual in its original packaging
in the back corner of the room, the discourse of consumerism in overflow-
ing bins of scissors, glue sticks, markers, and full-length pencils in bright
red plastic tubs in expensive blond wood cubbies). Given the profusion of
concretized and verbalized discourses in any given place, the key is to dis-
cover which discourses are foregrounded and which are backgrounded in
the interactions among social actors in that place, in this case, the children
playing in the classroom. The most backgrounded discourses are also most
powerful: naturalized expectations that operate "invisibly" (or perhaps in-
audibly) at the level of actions, integrated into nexuses of practice where
they circulate as just the natural way of doing things (Scollon & Scollon,
2004). I suggest that in classrooms, discourses circulate through routines,
daily automatic practices that every substitute teacher recognizes through
the familiar objection, "But that's not how you're *supposed* to do it."

Routines are part of the web of nexus that creates the fabric of everyday social participation, engaging in ways of belonging in a community of
practice. Rather than regulating children's minds and bodies (Boldt, 2001)
through accountability discourse admonitions for closely controlled behavior, quiet voices, and orderly work spaces, nurturing discourse in Abbie's
routines attended to children's physical, social, and emotional needs: need
to play, need for protection, and need for activity matched to a developmental stage articulated in developmentally appropriate practice (Bredekamp,
1987; Bredekamp & Copple, 1997).

The activity system behind the nurturing discourse in this kindergarten's
nexus of practice positions children (subjects) as developing learners who
invent their own literacy (outcome) through exploration and play (tools)
within print-rich and responsive environments (objects) in a developmental
progression (rules) toward conventional forms (Ferreiro & Teberosky, 1982;
Tolchinsky, 2003). Developmentally appropriate practitioners are to protect
children from inappropriately difficult or abstract tasks that might interrupt
development (International Reading Association & National Association for
the Education of Young Children, 1998, 2009; Neuman & Roskos, 2005).
However, this ostensibly agentic discourse also limits children and teachers.

Nurturing requires needy subjects; children are positioned as innocents who need teachers (women) who suggest rather than direct, teach by facilitating, protect, and comfort. Feminist poststructuralist research points out paradoxes that women face in fulfilling contradictory educational ideals of passive nurturer and strong advocate (Cannella, 2000; Grieshaber & Cannella, 2001; Walkerdine, 1994). Nurturing discourse diminishes opportunities for young girls, imposing identity expectations for cooperation and passivity; girls are interpreted as teacher helpers who work while boys are interpreted as active explorers who learn (Davies & Saltmarsh, 2007; Nichols, 2002; Walkerdine, 1990). Of course, many critical researchers argue that teachers and children also act as agents who strategically use discourse and are not mere dupes of institutional systems (Blaise, 2005b; Boldt, 2002; Britzman, 1991; Thorne, 1993). Just like Emma and Lubna, other Abbie Wannabes ingeniously invoked power by imagining and enacting nurturing but powerful play identities (e.g., teacher, mother), thereby expanding their access to a wider range of available practices and opportunities as they wielded developmentally appropriate practices and routines to position other children.

A NEW BASIS FOR PLAY IN EARLY LITERACY CLASSROOMS

Ironically, at a time when educational researchers are reconceptualizing and expanding what counts as literacy to include multimodal ways of knowing, governmental policies rely on constricted definitions of literacy and achievement (Siegel, 2006). Rather than recognizing the imaginative power of children's play as a literacy that expands meanings and encourages collaboration, recent accountability measures (e.g., No Child Left Behind in the United States) challenge kindergarten and primary teachers to justify play activities within an increasingly academic curriculum. Yet in this play-intensive classroom, Abbie reported that every child in her class exceeded the school district's end-of-year literacy benchmarks that identified children for remedial services in 1st grade (personal communication).

Given widespread accountability pressures, how is it that Abbie was able to provide such a play-rich learning environment? Abbie built support for her innovative teaching through parent partnerships. Although parents are often skeptical about the benefits of play-based learning (Goldstein, 2007), I witnessed strong support for Abbie and her teaching among the children's families. From the beginning of the school year, Abbie actively worked *with* parents as partners, cultivating a caring classroom community that included families, using newsletters not just to inform parents but to consult and recruit them, communicating weekly with each child's family, and encouraging parents to share their expertise to enrich kindergarten inquiry themes. Although Abbie felt compelled to comply with district mandates to use a commercial literacy program during daily shared reading sessions, she structured the majority of the morning literacy block to allow children to choose their activities and projects. It's important to acknowledge that Abbie's principal played a key role in allowing teachers the agency to use the commercial curriculum as a resource rather than requiring teachers to be regulated by it. This administrative flexibility made it possible for Abbie to design a play-based literacy curriculum that was challenging, responsive, and inclusive.

CHAPTER THREE

"Just Playin' Around" and "Just Makin' Stuff" to Make a Space for Just Guys

"I'm just drawin'." Marshall, a slight blond boy in a cotton baseball jersey and an Ivy League haircut, angles his green marker at 45 degrees and arcs it back and forth, laying down wide swaths of color on what will be a Teenage Mutant Ninja Turtle. Next to him, Dustin, a muscular kindergartner with buzzed tawny hair in a nylon mesh football jersey, arranges SpongeBob stick puppets on his partially completed storyboard.

As Dustin draws another puppet character, he stops and offers his pencil, "Marshall, can you draw a Cubs thing [team logo] on here for me?"

Lubna approaches the table clutching her writer's notebook, her thick black hair pulled into a long braid punctuated by a satiny pink bow. She overhears Dustin's request, and states matter-of-factly, "I hate Cubs."

The boys react immediately and simultaneously. Marshall is incredulous, "You don't like the Cubs?" and Dustin is curious, "You like the Red Sox?" As the children draw and color, they talk to determine who likes/hates the Cubs, the Red Sox, the White Sox, and other baseball teams.

After a few minutes, Lubna steps away from the table to gather magazine pictures for the *I Spy* book she is making, Dustin turns and taps Marshall's marker lightly with his own marker. The tap is an invitation to engage in a *Star Wars* duel, and a pivot that turns the boys' plastic markers into light sabers, "You're Darth Maul and I'm Darth Vader. This is [just] practice because we're both on the bad side."

The boys are fencing when Lubna returns, "Are you guys talking about Darth Vader over there? I want to work, okay? I want to work, I said."

Dustin and Marshall laugh but also turn back to their drawings.

JUST GUYS, LITERACY, AND THE BOY PROBLEM

A prevailing view interprets this snippet of activity as evidence of "the boy problem" (c.f., Sax, 2007), a persistent issue that constructs boys' interests and activity as incompatible with school (Connolly, 2004; Newkirk, 2002). In this interpretation, Marshall and Dustin became bored with writing workshop and took a break from drawing sports logos to play around in a *Star Wars* mock fight. And even when they did schoolwork, the boys drew cartoon characters, in general, doing what they could to avoid writing. In contrast, Lubna dutifully worked on a school-sanctioned task by pasting and labeling pictures in order to create a guessing game book to read to the class. Further, she enacted a "teacher's helper" role typical of Abbie Wannabes. Playing the teacher, she questioned the boys' "off-task" behavior and stressed her intention to work, getting them back on track. In this view, girls' interests already align neatly with school goals but boys need extra attention and special curricula infused with popular media and technologies in order to hold their interest (Fletcher, 2006).

In this book, I take a different perspective. Rather than interpreting this activity as a fixed set of traits, behaviors, or interests unique to boys, I situate the children's literacy play in a nexus of practice, that is, the gender practices and dispositions inscribed in habitus in early childhood. The boys' design[1] and play practices formed a nexus shaped by models of boyhood circulated through global discourses in schooling, gender, and popular media. I argue that when these emergent sports fans came to kindergarten, they used this nexus of literacy practices to appropriate materials to make their own toys and cordon off a play space for enacting masculinities.

Just Guys—Marshall and Dustin along with Adam, Matt, Patrick, and Scott—regularly drew pictures and constructed toys while playing during reading and writing workshop. I named this play group of six White boys "Just Guys" to reflect the all-male makeup of the group but also because they often denied that the images or toys they produced held any meaning. The boys characterized their products as "just a design" and their practices as "just drawin' somethin'" or "just playin' around." However, Just Guys did more than play around: Their pretense imagined out-of-school events into school space, replaced teacher mediation with peer mediation, and maintained hierarchical mentoring relationships in a boys-only space. When Just Guys did attach meanings to their creations, they drew upon sporting events or favorite male popular culture characters such as Ninja Turtles, Spider-Man, Darth Vader, or SpongeBob SquarePants. The boys often dressed in local university colors and talked about team sports as they "made stuff" and coached each other on art projects. "Makin' stuff" involved creating two-dimensional images and three-dimensional artifacts by folding and cutting paper, stringing beads into necklaces, mixing paints on the easel, or gluing feathers, fabric scraps, paints, glue, and a variety of papers in free-form collages.

The previous chapter showed how Abbie's kindergarten operated as a literacy apprenticeship and how Abbie Wannabes used tacit practices in literacy play nexus to transform their classroom identities. This chapter examines how Just Guys layered design practices, meanings, and identities in literacy play nexus into drawings and paper toys that enhanced their status in both classroom cultures. Drawings and artifacts were crafted through intense peer collaboration in a boys-only space, complicated by tensions among discourses of gender and schooling circulating in this kindergarten apprenticeship.

I used multimodal analysis (Jewitt, 2006; Norris, 2004) to look at play and design for multimodality, the interplay among material aspects of the environment that can be used for making meaning, and to understand how combinations of modes such as gaze, image, print, speech, or gesture in children's play or designs affect the meanings children can make (Jewitt & Kress, 2003; Kress, 2003a). (See Appendix C for an explanation and extended example of multimodal discourse analysis.) Following an overview of Just Guys' typical play and design practices, two examples from the playing/designing nexus illustrate how modes cluster during artifact production in school. In the first event, Just Guys used image, sound effects, action, and gesture as they drew sports logos and mascots to reproduce a football game and carry off identities as true sports fans. In the second event, Marshall layered modes and design expertise into a SpongeBob paper sack puppet as he explored the material affordances of masking tape by "playing around." Following these examples, close analysis of the boys' peer mediation in one episode shows how Just Guys competed as they helped each other make paper airplanes, and how their design prowess and sports knowledge served as cultural capital for gaining access, displaying skill inside the boys' group, building group cohesion, and closing off their play group to a girl. This analysis problematizes the notion of a "boy problem" and models of production that circulate through discourses of schooling, masculinities and competition.

PLAY, DESIGN, AND MULTIMODALITY

Multimodality (Jewitt & Kress, 2003) provides a way to critically examine literacies for layered practices, identities, modes, and discourses. Literacies, like all sign-making activity, always involve multiple modes but particular literacy practices tend to foreground particular modes (Kress, 1997):

- Talking and singing foreground verbal and auditory modes including speech, music, and sound effect.
- Reading, writing, and designing foreground visual modes, including print, image, gaze, and mediated action with books, writing tools, or art materials.
- Playing foregrounds action modes, including gesture, posture, movement, and mediated action with props or proxies such as dolls and puppets.

Multimodality fuels the representational power of literacies by providing multiple avenues for changing the meaning of a sign by making it with different materials, also changing what meanings can be made and who gets access.

Playing with Meanings and Materials

Enacting identities and animating toys

In order to enact pretend identities or to animate toys and objects, children recontextualize here-and-now meanings, that is, they detach the conventional meaning attached to a physical object in the local context and reattach a different meaning to produce a sign better suited to their play scenario (Vygotsky, 1935/1978). Through play, any material object in the classroom can be transformed to create a new sign, including toys—commercial or child-made—or literacy materials such as pens, paints, and paper. For example, Dustin transformed his marker into a light saber to enact Darth Vader. The light saber's play meaning is shaped not only by Dustin's intended purpose (to play Darth Vader) but also by the physical properties of the available marker. A plastic marker bears an iconic (Peirce in Hartshorne, Weiss, & Burks, 1998) resemblance to a plastic toy light saber that makes it a plausible substitute: It's cylindrical, narrow, yet substantial enough to make a satisfying clicking sound when hit against another marker. Dustin and Marshall shared an unspoken understanding that the marker tap was a sign, an invitation to play, a pivot that recontextualized the classroom as a film scene and writing tools as light sabers in a duel between two *Star Wars* villains. This instantaneous shared meaning was accomplished nonverbally through the mediated action of a marker tap. Such tacit recognition is the hallmark of the backgrounded, valued practices that mark membership and elicit the automatic cooperation of members within a particular community of practice (Scollon, 2001b), in this case demonstrating the boys' knowledge of light saber dueling, science-fiction media, and their identities as *Star Wars* fans. Recontextualizing space expanded meanings and participation opportunities by bringing present and non-present worlds together: the immediate world of the classroom with an imagined or remembered world that indexed another time and space (Bateson, 1955/1972; Goffman, 1974).

Animation transformed artifacts into props or toys with intensified meanings, whether as props that carried double meanings (e.g., the real marker and the simulated light saber) or as proxies that allowed the child to animate double identities (e.g., the imagined pilot in the paper airplane and the flyer/animator who sails the plane across the classroom).

Exploring material meanings

> At the art table, several kindergartners are drawing their faces, stopping now and then to peer seriously into the individual metal mirrors scattered around the table. All except Scott. Instead of drawing the expected self-portrait, he colors with a gray crayon, moving it furiously back and forth across the white page. Pressing very hard, he transforms his paper into a smooth waxy gray surface. Impressed, I comment, "Wow, that looks just like the mirror." Absorbed in his work, he nods slightly, "Yeah." Dustin leans across the table to get a better look at Scott's "mirror."

Scott's coloring produced a *motivated* sign, that is, a sign designed to exploit the physical properties and cultural meanings of materials to further the sign-maker's social interest (Kress, 1997). Children strategically manipulated materials to make motivated signs, inspired by the sensory qualities of available materials. While other children used the metal mirrors and wax crayons as literacy tools to create images of themselves, Scott focused on representing the material similarities of the objects he held in his hands: the sheen in the waxiness of crayons and the shininess of the mirror. Young children are attracted to (or in some discourses of schooling, distracted by) such "robust materiality" in classroom materials in ways that deviate from teacher-endorsed uses (Bomer, 2003, p. 231). The transformational potential of literacy tools provided "affordances, both intended and unintended" (p. 223), allowing Dustin, Marshall, and Scott to use markers, crayons, and mirrors in unexpected ways that enhanced their intended meanings.

Children's explorations often traveled along a single mode of materiality: auditory exploration of the tinkling sounds made by tapping a hard plastic cup with a wooden stirrer, visual exploration of parallel lines drawn by holding two pencils, or kinesthetic exploration by rolling markers along a tabletop. Children played with auditory rhythms, words, and sounds as they read, stacked markers together to waggle ridiculously long markers as they wrote, and discovered all sorts of unorthodox uses for glue, staplers, and tape as they designed. This exploration led to new tool uses and expanded texts: talking into earphones, creating a nonsensical rhyming name for a friend, or adding serifs to letters after looking closely at the font in a picture book. Meanings were transformed, even if by accident, as children probed the properties of materials or examined the effects produced by novel uses of tools.

Designing and "Makin' Stuff"

Drawing images

Design transformed ideas into material forms that could carry durable messages to be shared and transported (Brandt & Clinton, 2002). Given the accessible and abundant supply of materials in this kindergarten classroom, it's important to point out that children most often chose markers, pencils, or crayons to create images by coloring or drawing on paper. Images are two-dimensional, inscribed upon a flat surface, creating visual displays organized spatially in a left-right and top-down hierarchal matrix (Kress & van Leeuwen, 1996).

Just Guys stretched meanings of drawings as they invented ways to visually represent challenging subjects. For example, Marshall represented movement by drawing multiple baseballs arcing over a baseball diamond to show the path and motion of a homerun. At times, Just Guys' drawings meshed with Abbie's writing workshop activities: Dustin drew books, storyboards and scripts that starred SpongeBob as a football player, including a puppet show and a sequel, "SpongeBob Goes to High School" and "SpongeBob Goes to College." Beyond showing their artistic ability, Just Guys' drawings demonstrated their knowledge of sports uniforms, logos, and athletic events. Dustin's drawing of a college football uniform included both the home and away jerseys while Adam's storyboard for a football game showed his understanding that the quarterback needs to find an open receiver. Drawings also demonstrated Just Guys' awareness of specific literacy practices and forms associated with college sports. During March, Adam and Dustin drew approximations of NCAA basketball tournament brackets and filled in their favorite teams on the blank lines.

Constructing artifacts

Children constructed artifacts when they cut out their drawings or folded papers to make paper airplanes. As children transformed flat images or materials into three-dimensional objects, they brought their drawn representations into the real world and increased their usefulness as artifacts in the "world of action" where play practices gave the constructed artifacts additional meanings (Kress, 1997). Children used multiple mediated actions with design tools as they constructed artifacts for play; in addition to drawing and coloring, popular mediated actions included:

- separating and cutting
- arranging and layering
- combining and affixing
- rolling and folding

SEPARATING AND CUTTING

Dustin stands next to the sink, waiting for the minute or so that it takes the class to line up for lunch. He pulls a palm-sized folded white paper with rounded corners out of his pocket, unfolds it and holds it to his ear. As he talks into this paper flip phone, its opened surface displays a grid of small squares that represent a numeric pad topped by a larger blank square that stands for a screen.

The mediated action *cutting* changes images into objects by producing an edge that establishes spatial boundaries and a shape that enables manipulation in three-dimensional reality (Kress, 1997). When Dustin drew a cell phone, he created an image that could be viewed; when he cut out this image, he turned the image into an artifact that could be used to talk to others, to signify coolness, and to create an affinity object (Fernie, Kantor, & Whaley, 1995), an object desired by other children used to display status and inspire imitation in the peer culture as a tangible sign of cultural capital. Dustin's cell phone was one of many Just Guys' paper crafts that simulated new technologies and that produced instant classroom fads, highly desirable and much-copied. As in many kindergartens, computers were unavailable so the boys often invented paper electronics such as paper iPods with yarn and pompon headphones.

ARRANGING AND LAYERING.

Marshall and Matt sit side-by-side as they weave nubby strands of red yarn on handheld cardboard looms. Abbie has made individual looms for each child, from matboard cut into 6"x 8" rectangles with white cotton strings threaded through the slots in the two longer sides. Marshall weaves and unravels, weaves and unravels as he works to thread the yarns, alternating over and under the white strings. Halfway finished, it's clear that although each of his individual red yarns alternates over and under the vertical strings, all of Marshall's rows match rather than alternate in a basket-weave pattern. Lin, a confident weaver whose deft over-under motions quickly filled her loom with alternating rows, now patiently snips 6-inch lengths of yarn for the other children who are not yet finished. Her offer, "Who wants blue?" prompts Marshall to wisecrack, "I need 100!" Jaeden asks, "How many do you need, Marshall, for real?" Marshall shoots back, "Okay, I need 99! 60 hundred, I need 2,000!"

Marshall used the mediated actions *layering* and *arranging* to construct a weaving. He used yarn weaving as a way to produce a pleasing display as well as a means to joke with others at the table during this challenging project. Whether the activity resulted in an artifact, an image, or an open-ended experiment, depended upon the meanings that children attached to projects. Some weavers at the table semiotized their projects as little blankets, others created "just designs," interesting aesthetic displays or explorations of ways that yarn strands fit together. These meanings were fluid and overlapping, changing from moment to moment within the course of the event. In similar ways, children inventively layered and arranged fabric and magazine cut-outs to produce collages or stacked blocks to build structures.

COMBINING AND AFFIXING.

Marshall tapes three strips of masking tape to a blank sheet of paper, forming an H. He then draws and colors a picture of SpongeBob, which makes the tape strips resemble suspenders. The tape begins to roll toward the edge of the table. Marshall catches it just as it begins to topple off. Marshall puts his other papers back into his writing folder, perhaps other puppets to be created. He talks to the papers as he places them in his folder, "I'm going to get you other guys out of the way now. Say Good-bye. Say Good-bye to your practice friend." As he closes his folder, Marshall explains, "This is not SpongeBob in my puppet show. I just made this one for fun."

Not surprisingly, the mediated actions *combining* and *affixing* often followed arranging and layering of materials to make projects permanent and portable. In this example, Marshall combined separate pieces of paper by affixing tape to paper to decorate or clothe a puppet. Children also used gluing, stapling, and sewing to combine two sections of a project or two kinds of materials to attach appendages or to make projects more durable.

ROLLING AND FOLDING.

> Adam, Jaeden, and Marshall are making "electric eels"
> that look uncannily like the *Star Wars* light sabers Marshall
> made a few weeks earlier. Each boy rolls a piece of white
> paper, starting at one corner and rolling on the diagonal to
> make a tube of paper with a point on both ends. Jaeden has
> difficulty rolling his paper diagonally, and starts over several
> times. Marshall silently rolls a tube of paper and hands it
> to Jaeden for taping, but the paper unrolls when placed
> on the table. Adam and Marshall secure the edges of their
> papers with tape and coloring jagged lines on the surface
> of the tubes. The two boys swim their electric eels over to
> a corner of the classroom, swooping the paper tubes in
> large oscillating waves. When it is time to clean up, Jaeden
> crumples his partially completed eel and throws it away;
> Adam and Marshall fence with the once-eels-now-swords
> until it is time to line up for lunch.

The mediated actions *rolling* and *folding* paper surpassed cutting for effectiveness in adding dimension to a two-dimensional image. Folding produced a depth and a reality that cutting alone could not achieve. Further, advanced folding techniques such as origami produced durable objects for play—games, doll clothing, and small animals that invited animation.

THE PLAYING/DESIGNING NEXUS

By combining design practices with play practices, Just Guys created images and artifacts that moved signs across visual, auditory, and kinesthetic modes. Making and animating a single artifact involved multiple mediated actions with varied media: for example, drawing a car, coloring or painting it, cutting it out, writing logos on it, making engine sounds, and pushing it along the floor. Children extend, enhance, and transform meanings through this process of transduction, moving a sign from mode to mode (Kress, 1997). Multimodality makes the playing/designing nexus an action-intensive space, dense with modes of production and a prime site for meaning and identity transformation.

Figure 3.1 maps the social space where play and design practices intersect in the Just Guys play group (shown as a white dotted oval) in relation to play and design practices in peer culture. Two lines represent the design practices *drawing* images and *constructing* artifacts (including layering, cutting, folding, affixing, and so on). One line represents the play practice *exploring* materials. The starred points indicate nexuses that link and integrate multiple design and play practices (that is, moments where practices co-occur purposefully). The close proximity of nexuses indicates the fluidity among overlapping practices, for example, the way children move minute-to-minute from drawing to constructing to animating when they drew pictures, cut them out, and played with the cut-outs in impromptu dramatizations.

The next section shows how Just Guys created drawings and paper toys and produced tangible evidence of their multimodal practices as well as their relational identities.

Figure 3.1. Just Guys in Playing/Designing Nexus

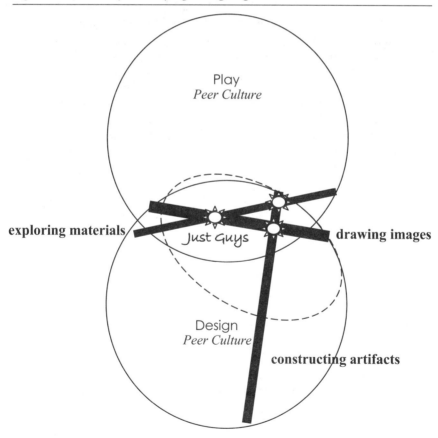

Designing to Play

Marshall shares his drawing of a "super-Eagle." This
variation on the Midwestern University mascot is a wingless
bird with a crescent head, "I comed at, on this idea,
awright?"

Matt and Patrick compliment Marshall—"Marshall's a
good draw-er, you know"—and ask him to draw a super-
Eagle on each of their papers. Matt watches intently as
Marshall forms a triangular shape on his paper but Patrick
is engrossed in smacking one marker against another to
see whether it will roll or spin, depending upon where
he strikes it. He hits the marker at rhythmic intervals and
chants, "Let's go Midwe:stern! Whoop woo-whoop! Let's
go Midwe::stern! Whoop woo-whoop!"

Marshall responds, "Wet's go MidWe::stern." He points
to his drawing and throws his arm upward: "Yeah baby—
Ya:H!" He holds a marker close to his chest and strums it as
an air guitar.

Matt leans across the table to ask Patrick, "Hey,
'member when those—when the Eagles weren't doing so
good. Everyone who hated the Eagles were going for [the
other team]. And then remember what happened? [cupping
his hands around his mouth and lowering the pitch of his
voice] "Boo::o. Boo:o. Boo:o."

Patrick: That was *not* good.
Matt: Yeah, I was at that game. I was.
Patrick [stops hitting the marker and looks up]: You were?
Matt: I was.
Patrick: Coach was there.
Matt: He was?
Patrick: I wasn't. Were you on July 10th? Were you at July
    10th? 'Cause we were at July 10th.

Marshall, Matt, and Patrick drew and colored super-Eagles with care,
repeatedly consulting one another on the design and placement of each figure
(Figure 3.2). As in Scott's drawing of a mirror, visual analysis of the boys'
designs shows their attention to the effects of color, texture, and form in their
representations. Intent on getting the colors and symbols exactly right, the
boys reproduced team colors: yellow/black for Eagles' mascots and red/blue
for Cubs logos. Matt pressed hard with fresh markers to create saturated
red, blue, yellow, and black rather than pastels that would be produced by

lightly scribbling with colored pencils. The diagonal orientation of Matt's super-Eagle, copied and embellished from Marshall's design, created a sense of motion and drama (Jewitt & Oyama, 2001), an ascending bird flying into two descending super-Eagles, perhaps moments after a collision. Later, Abbie helped the boys transduct their play enactments of sports fans into modes and forms of valued school literacy practices, encouraging them to write and draw books of recent sports events; label diagrams of baseball diamonds, football fields, scoreboards, and team uniforms; and write scripts for football iMovies.

Analysis of the boys' gestures and mediated actions reveals the transformative effects of play on the meanings in their designs. When Matt cupped his hands to animate his drawing with the gesture and sound effect of a booing fan and Marshall strummed a marker as an air guitar, the meanings of their drawings and tools shifted. Animation transformed Matt's image into a re-enactment of an event and Marshall's marker into a toy with intensified meanings—a prop that carried double meanings (e.g., real marker and simulated guitar).

Figure 3.2. Super-Eagle Drawing

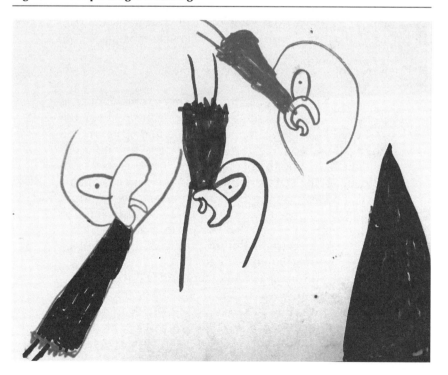

The chanting, marker spinning, air guitar strumming, crowd booing gestures, and sound effects in this play event show that contrary to their claims, the three boys did more than "just draw" and more was at stake than the creation of an aesthetically pleasing picture. Stepping back to look at the boys' group activity as recontextualization, the boys combined modes of image, gaze, gesture, and accompanying sports talk to reference past games, thus making distant events available as sites for displaying knowledge and bonding through recollection of shared experiences. Layering other time-spaces onto present situations is a powerful discursive device that expands meanings and opportunities for positioning others (Leander, 2004; Wohlwend, 2007a). The boys' attempts to verbally locate themselves at the same past football games further strengthened the cohesion of the boys' group and legitimated their individual identities as "real" sports fans who attended actual sporting events.

Just Guys gained stature within their group by incorporating sports trademarks (such as mascots, Cubs logo, university name) into their designs and football chants into their storytelling, drawing, and writing. The boys also used their super-Eagles drawings to rank each other and demonstrate their relative design skills. Matt and Patrick admired Marshall's drawing ability and his sports expertise, evident in their compliments and requests to have him draw on their papers, actions that established him as artistic expert and group leader. To develop this expertise, Marshall frequently explored art materials and tools, as in the following example.

Playing (Around) to Design

Marshall positions a pair of scissors in one hand, using his chest to steady the scissors as he puts his fingers in the grips. Cradling the roll of masking tape under his arm, he takes his fingers out of the grips of the scissors and uses both hands to open the blades with a jerk. He repositions his fingers in the scissors, unwinds about 5 inches of tape and clips off a 3-inch piece of tape, and sets the scissors on the table. The tape curls and twists back on itself and he cannot straighten out the tape strip. He attaches a sticky-side-out tape loop to the left top corner of the rectangle, flattening it down with his fingers.

Marshall turns the wheel of tape, finds the end, and peels back another 3-inch strip of tape. This time, he cuts the tape strip close to place where the tape leaves the roll. He attaches the tape sticky-side-down to his paper below the tape loop and smoothes the piece of tape with his hands so that it lies flat on the paper.

He then unrolls another strip of tape, this time placing the tape roll between his knees to steady the tape as he pulls back a 2-inch strip and clips it off, but it twists and sticks to the scissors.

Marshall uses his newly invented method of holding the tape roll between his knees to cut another piece of tape. This time he pins down the tape with his thumb so that it doesn't tangle.

Holding the scissors in his right hand, Marshall pulls tape away from roll with his left hand. He suspends the roll by the strip of tape. He lifts the tape and tries to cut the tape with the scissor blades perpendicular to the tape edges but the blades of the scissors pinch the sticky edges of the tape together. He pulls the scissors back so that the edges unstick, causing the tape roll to twist back and forth.

Marshall stands up and holds the tape edge in one hand with the tape roll hanging free. He cuts the tape but this time, positions the blades parallel to the tape surface, allowing a clean cut. The tape roll drops upright on the table with a plop. Marshall smiles and sings a wordless tune, the *Stars Wars* theme, "ERR-err-err-err-ERRRRRR-err. ERR-err-err-ERRRRRR-err," as he smoothes the final piece of tape on the paper, attaching a second column of tape to his paper.

He picks up the tape again and unwinds the longest piece of tape yet, about 7 inches. The end of the tape immediately curls back upon itself and Marshall tries to untangle it. He announces, "I always draw. Even I play on my computer."

Marshall holds up tape and watches as the roll swings and twirls. He bends his head forward against the exposed sticky side of the tape strip. The tape adheres to his hair from his crown to his hairline. The tape roll bounces against his forehead and Marshall smiles. He picks up the scissors to cut the tape against his forehead, changes his mind and begins pulling off the tape. The tape pulls at his hair as he removes it. "Ow. Ow, ow, ow, ow, ow." Pulling the tape completely free, Marshall sits up, glances at the nearby teacher associate, looks at me and grins, "A:::h-ow:::.."

Still holding the scissors, he inspects the tape strip that he just pulled off his hair.

Marshall continues to experiment with various ways of holding the tape and scissors, pausing to attach a strip of tape horizontally across the two columns, creating an "H"

out of masking tape on his paper sack. Finally, holding the
tape above the table, he cuts at an angle parallel to its sticky
surface and snips off the tape, letting the tape roll fall to the
table. "Cut! Phew!"

Marshall then concentrates on drawing and coloring
SpongeBob with watercolor markers. He experiments, using
a red watercolor marker to cover the tape's water-resistant
surface. He tentatively drags an index finger across the wet
watercolor, and inspects the pinkish smudge that results.
He continues to smudge the tape until the entire surface of
the tape is pink instead of red. "I'm just playing around. I'm
just pre— I'm just play, playing around so, so I could draw
SpongeBob."

Marshall discovers the masking function of the tape
as he peels a corner of the tape away from the puppet
leaving a white space where the reddish tape had been. He
continues to peel off tape, holding the puppet down with
his left hand while peeling with his right. A passing child
asks, "Why you ripping that off?" "Because, so, so I will
want to know what it looks like. Who:::a. I [xxx] go looking
'at good. Hey!" As flickering lights signal cleanup, Marshall
shakes tape off his finger onto the table. "Get here. Ack."
He peels the last piece off the puppet but it catches the
edge of the paper and starts to rip the paper. Short on time,
he decides to stop with the last piece of tape on the top
right corner still attached. "That's okay. I'll just leave it."
Marshall tucks SpongeBob upside down into his writing
folder. "I like to study a bit."

Marshall spent 15 minutes cutting and sticking strips of tape as he
explored its adhesive properties and created a SpongeBob "practice"
puppet "just for fun," that is, a test case for a "real" puppet that he
might make in the future (Figure 3.3). Before he finished this practice
puppet, Marshall tested 14 techniques for cutting tape strips from a roll
of masking tape and developed his skills with tape and scissors. He also
experimented with its primary functions: water-resistance that protected
the paper from the red water-based marker and adhesiveness to various
surfaces, including his own hair.

Along with layers of paper, tape, and coloring, Marshall's habitus sedimented into the SpongeBob puppet during its production (Rowsell & Pahl,
2007). Whether a pencil, stapler, textbook, or roll of tape, a tool indexes a
specific cultural history that defines not only how the tool should be used
and for what purpose but also how the tool-user should behave (Bomer,

2003; Leont'ev, 1977; Vygotsky, 1935/1978). However, Marshall's play with scissors and tape enabled exploration and the discovery of new uses for tools that he could use to impress his peers. The sedimented layers in this child-made artifact chronicle his identities (Rowsell & Pahl, 2007) as an innovator and explorer, as a master kindergarten designer with advanced cutting and taping skills, as a peer mentor who could teach these skills to other kindergartners, as a fan of a cartoon series that features humor and parody of adults, and as a SpongeBob animator and puppeteer.

Modes layered into the puppet as well. Marshall changed his *posture* frequently, hunching over to pin the tape roll between his knees, extending his arm to watch the roll twirl above the table. He used the *mediated actions* cutting, coloring, and affixing to manipulate the scissors, markers, and tape. He *touched* the tape to his hair to test the stickiness of its surface. He used

Figure 3.3. Marshall's SpongeBob Practice Puppet

visual modes to *gaze* at the puppet and to draw and color an *image*. He used auditory modes of *music* and *speech* to hum a *Star Wars* tune and to talk to the stick puppets he had drawn ("Say goodbye. Say goodbye to your practice friends,") thereby animating their characters.

Play and design practices produced a modally dense (Norris, 2004) artifact that acted as a durable and portable text (Brandt & Clinton, 2002). Modal layers in the puppet included:

- verbal histories (remembered and invented storylines and dialogue for the SpongeBob character)
- tactile and visual properties (smooth paper, bright colors, hand-sized structure)
- past and future tool uses (prior use as a paper sack transformed into potential use as a hand puppet, realized uses of tape, scissors, and markers)
- mediated actions (object handling that increased Marshall's cutting and taping knowledge and skill development)

These sedimented modes and the quality of the artifact's design provided tangible evidence of Marshall's design skill and turned a paper puppet into a concrete marker of his identity as a master designer and a member of the Just Guys.

Using the device of "just for practice," Marshall created a teacher-free space to explore several design tools as he created a SpongeBob puppet. *Just for practice* suggests an aimlessness that protects children's space by deflecting instructional attempts to infuse print literacy into play activity: How can a child be expected to write a story, caption a picture, or label an image that is "just a design" with no attached meaning? An artifact created for practice is disposable, risk-free, and invites experimentation with techniques. In this kindergarten, learner exploration was valued and encouraged; however, in many time-crunched classrooms in this standards-driven era, playing around with design is discouraged, even penalized. In such classrooms, playful exploration of materials and tools only occurs in the cracks of the daily schedule, when the teacher isn't watching.

Rethinking children's designed artifacts as texts with sedimented modes, practices, and identities (Pahl & Rowsell, 2010) recognizes the meanings communicated through drawings, crafts, and art projects—even those created just for practice. Children strategically craft these objects, which in turn shape their identities as they select materials for the physical properties and design affordances that influence how their texts are used and read. The complexity of these texts suggests the need to closely examine artifacts in their sites of production in order to read their layered assemblages of meanings, practices, modes, and discourses.

MULTIMODALITY AND MEDIATION
IN THE PLAYING/DESIGNING NEXUS

Marshall takes a paper to the writing table. He quickly makes straight folds, matching up the lines very carefully and smoothing the paper to make sharp creases.

Finished, he takes his first paper airplane to Abbie, who is kneeling next to Matt to admire his latest drawing. "Look what I can make. I know how to make them now."

Abbie asks Marshall how he learned to make paper airplanes. "My dad showed me." Marshall demonstrates by folding a new sheet of paper on the carpet. He discards the paper halfway through when one of the folds does not line up correctly but after this false start, successfully folds a second airplane.

Impressed, Abbie makes several suggestions, "Wow, you did it! You know, Marshall, that would be a great thing for you to do. You could make a how-to book at Writers' Workshop time. . . . You could almost write those directions down just like you showed me. Then you could teach the kids. You could make it a choice [center that Marshall could direct]."

Lin, watching from the nearby sand table, notices Abbie's interest in the boys' paper airplane folding. Lin is a Chinese-American girl who shares the boys' avid interest in design and university sports but usually plays by herself, a few feet away from the Just Guys.

The boys return to the table. Matt holds up a sheet of paper, folded in half. "Now what do you do?"

Marshall reaches across and begins to make the next fold for Matt but Matt pulls the paper away, "Hey, stop, *I'm* makin' it!"

Marshall directs Matt through the next step by pointing and touching the places where the paper should be folded. He adds somewhat vague directions intended to be helpful, "Matt, you do it on another part and then you need to snip it."

Lin walks up to the writing table but neither boy acknowledges her. She watches them for a few moments, gets a blank sheet of paper from the nearest shelf, sits in the child-sized blue rocker in the center of the room, and begins folding an airplane, smoothing the creases against her lap.

Midway through the process, Adam, a member of the Just Guys group, approaches the pair, "What're you makin'?"

"Airplane."

Adam objects, "But Mrs. Howard won't let us."

Marshall explains that Abbie wants the boys to demonstrate how to make the planes and Adam quickly gets a sheet of paper to start his own airplane.

Adam stands at the end of the table folding his paper on his own as Marshall continues to teach Matt. After each step, Matt questions, "Now what do you do?" (The step-by-step peer mediation that Marshall provides to help Matt make one airplane is closely examined in Appendix C.)

After making the last fold of his own plane, Marshall leaves the table to show his third airplane to the nearby teaching assistant. As he returns, Adam stops him to show off the plane he invented: the "best paper airplane ever," its random folds pointing out in every direction.

Back at the table, the three boys continue to fold paper as they compare and evaluate their airplanes.

After finishing a fourth plane, Marshall leaves the table but Matt follows him and hands his plane to Marshall. Puzzled, Marshall inspects Matt's misfolded plane but cannot see what to do next. He laughs, "What? How did I...?"

A few feet away, Lin sits skillfully folding a much more intricate paper airplane with wider wings but the boys do not notice it nor does she show it to them.

Matt returns to the writing table and makes the final fold on his plane. Meanwhile, Marshall pretends to fly his plane around the room as he shows it to other children including Lin who glances at it.

When Lin finishes her own plane, she takes it to the teacher associate who smiles and chats with her. Lin walks on, stops momentarily at the sand table, and then walks back to teacher associate, "I folded it." She gives the plane a toss and it glides about ten feet before drifting into a counter.

Marshall moves to the carpet and folds a fifth plane. Adam kneels next to him and critiques the plane's design. "That one just slip slops around. It does. My grandma made it before. As Marshall makes the last fold, he hands the plane to Adam, "Here. You can have that one if you want it. Have it!"

Adam accepts with a doubtful, "Does it fly good?"

"Um, a little bit, OK?" Adam loops the plane, pretending to fly it with large swooping circles, "Does it go like this? Loop-ba, loop-ba, loop-ba, loop-ba." Together, Adam and Marshall pretend to fly the plane over to the locker area. When they reach the classroom wall, they test out the plane by tossing it back across the classroom. When the plane glides and sinks after about eight feet, Adam concedes, "That flies really good."

After finally finishing a plane, Matt decorates it with flames while Marshall embellishes his own plane. Marshall uses masking tape to attach two popsicle stick handles onto the bottom edge of the plane which he then carries around like a placard. Adam returns to the table to make another paper airplane with invented fan-like folds.

Marshall calls me over and directs me to document each step in his plane folding process, "Take a picture each time I do something to make a paper airplane....Then somebody will know how to make one." (See Figure 3.4 for a page from the book that Marshall wrote using these photographs the next week during writing workshop. (Text reads, "Fold it again.")

Making Stuff (and Exclusionary Space) through Peer Mediation

When Marshall coached Matt's paper folding, the boys established an insider activity, protected by the value that they gave to paper airplanes that followed a particular set of design conventions for construction. Each fold of the airplane provided evidence of the boys' ability to comply with a set of steps and to complete a shared design so that the finished aircraft was 1) a badge that represented its designers' level of expertise and his status as a group member and 2) a toy to use to enter into an airplane-flying enactment with other Just Guys. (See Appendix C for close analysis of modes, action, and talk during a 3 minute segment excerpted from this 21 minute paper airplane episode.)

Adam's objection to making paper airplane, "But Mrs. Howard won't let us," highlights its reputation as a dubious school activity. At best, paper airplanes are valued in peer culture but are only peripherally related to school-sanctioned literacy practices. However, Abbie opened an opportunity for merging peer and school cultures by creating a link between the boys' interest in airplane folding and the practice of authoring within the structure of Writers' Workshop: She encouraged Marshall to write a "how-to" book, which turned the paper-folding into a pre-writing activity. In the Just Guys

Figure 3.4. A Page from Marshall's Book *How to Fold a Paper Airplane*

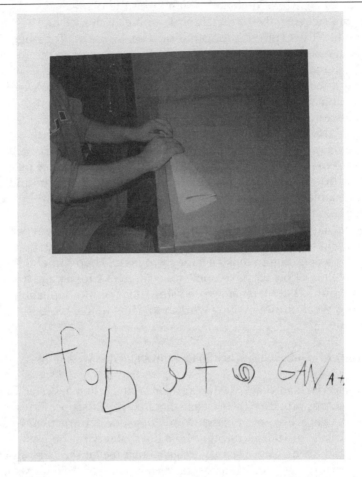

group, Marshall wrote sentences for each page with a digital photo to create a step-by-step sequence of directions; Adam stapled actual samples of paper airplanes at each step into his airplane book.

The SpongeBob puppet and paper airplane activities show that playful exploration created opportunities for participation as well as knowledge-building and skill development. Not all of the children in the Just Guys groups displayed Marshall's advanced artistic ability; some children simply copied his designs or drew very simple representations in order to have op-portunities to connect with the other boys in the group. Whether Just Guys created or copied designs, they all engaged in design practices for social purposes, developing and honing skills in order to be recognized as members of the play group.

The Just Guys' peer mediation strengthened group cohesion by acting and talking a space into being, creating a place in the classroom for playing and designing their own projects that appeared disconnected from typical goals of school literacy such as producing books or writing in journals. Their shared practices developed group cohesion through four peer culture concerns: constructing a gendered identity, resisting adult culture, exercising power through status within the group, and developing group inclusion through the protection of interactive space (Kyratzis, 2004). However, a cohesive group upholds a boundary, creating insiders, outsiders, and issues of exclusion. Even in this classroom where children were expected to collaborate and mediate for each other, access to groups was not distributed equally. The boys shared a history of working together with shared expectations and interaction patterns that excluded Lin, who had a history of working alone and outside the group. In a community of practice, power can be wielded through exclusion as certain individuals are held on the periphery (Scollon, 2001b) and denied the scripts, or accepted ways of representing, which provide greater access to privileged status within a particular community (Gutiérrez, Rymes, & Larson, 1995). Even though Lin possessed the ability to independently produce a paper airplane, she was ignored and excluded by the boys, not through verbal scripts but nonverbally through the direction of gaze, absence of talk, and a shared way of folding paper.

Opening Exclusionary Space through Teacher Mediation

Abbie actively worked to interrupt children's exclusionary tactics in several ways that eventually contributed to Lin's inclusion in the boys' group by the end of the school year. Abbie valued children's diverse home literacies and sought ways for parents and children to share their cultural expertise. She provided classroom time and space for children to share their out-of-school passions and to teach other children. When Abbie saw that Lin was excluded from the boys' group, she drew upon Lin's expertise and the boys' design interests to create opportunities for Lin to teach interested children—including Marshall, Adam, and Matt—how to create other paper projects. As Lin taught children to fold Japanese origami and to write Chinese characters, she demonstrated skills that provided cultural capital that enabled her to join in more easily at the Just Guys' table.

Abbie's mediation proved cyclical, generative, and culturally responsive. To inspire Marshall and other children to write books, Abbie provided examples of the how-to genre by adding illustrated instruction books to the classroom library. In this way, she embedded a design practice valued in the peer culture within a school literacy practice. This also stretched the activity of paper folding by linking to its cross-cultural history in origami. Abbie added several origami how-to books—many step-by-step and a few bilingual—to the supply of books in the classroom library and displayed on counters around the room. These origami books provided models for child-authored how-to books and new designs to inspire further folded paper projects. By embedding the boys' airplane folding within origami and legitimating both as appropriate school projects, Abbie also validated Mei Yu and Lin's interest in Japanese origami and accessed the girls' knowledge about Chinese and Japanese cultures. Over the course of the next month, origami projects and how-to books proliferated and Lin assumed a leadership role in teaching other children, especially Adam, several complex origami designs.

MULTIMODALITY AND DISCOURSES OF PRODUCTION

The interaction among Marshall, Matt, Adam, Lin, and Abbie shows that it is not enough to access and use multimodal resources; these uses must be recognized as valid ways of belonging according to the discourses that circulate in classroom cultures.

> The conflation and intersection of Discourses become modalities in texts, which, alongside practices, provide a formative picture of the meaning makers—not only their pathway into literacy but also how they make meaning in certain contexts and engage in practice. The theory provides a lens on *how* producers sediment identities and *what* identities they sediment. (Rowsell & Pahl, 2007, p. 392, emphasis in original)

The notion that texts bear tangible traces of the discourses that justified their production practices and modes offers an opportunity to track discourses behind classroom materials and Just Guys' artifacts. Several overlapping discourses in this kindergarten supported children's production of texts and artifacts—in complementary as well as contradictory ways.

Discourses of Schooling

The discourse of accountability and standardization calls for a quality control approach to education that ensures reliable production of high-achieving students. One goal of national standardization of schooling is to turn out a workforce capable of competing in a global marketplace. In an information era, this means workers with technical expertise who learn new skills quickly and flexibly adapt to changing conditions (Gee, 1996; New

London Group, 1996). We could reasonably expect that one outcome of this discourse would be that early childhood classrooms would be equipped with new technologies so that from the beginning of their school careers, children could learn to use 21st-century media. Ironically, the reverse is true: An emphasis on accountability and standardization has prompted a regressive move to drill and memorization and a reduction in the flexible problem-solving and critical thinking that the discourse promotes. Perhaps this should not be surprising as discourses often create effects that contradict their rhetoric, at times intentionally producing misrecognition (Bourdieu, 1982/1991). In any case, accountability discourse stresses verbal modes and print media in order to prepare students for annual, even semi-annual, standardized testing on literacy and numeracy skills.

Just Guys showed awareness of accountability discourse when they attended to the need to produce and display completed work as a necessary school task: showing finished airplanes to Abbie and to the teacher associate, creating a book from the airplane folding project to comply with Abbie's suggestion. Their preferred medium—paper—also reflected the medium of choice in accountability discourse. However, their mediated actions with paper created products not valued within accountability discourse. The primacy of action modes—folding, taping, cutting, animating, enacting, moving—in Just Guys' playful production of images and artifacts resisted the print-centric, serious, and silent seatwork expected within this discourse, the kind of work that Lubna insisted upon in the opening example in this chapter.

A discourse of personal expression circulated through the writing workshop approach that Abbie used to encourage children to produce books and drawings in daily writing sessions. In writing workshop, teachers model writing techniques so that children can think and act like adult writers in order to produce books. However, children are expected to write with their own "voice" to personally express their feelings or recount lived events (Newkirk, 1989). Children are expected to produce personal texts on a daily basis, rough drafts or journal entries collected in a writer's notebook, with the goal of polishing selected pieces into a "published" book; the emphasis is on quality of expression in order to produce a final version for the classroom library. This discourse privileges the verbal modes of speech, print, gaze, and the mediated action handwriting, putting letters on paper with pencils. Drawing is valued as a way to illustrate pages but print is foregrounded.

Just Guys were highly aware of the emphasis on verbal modes, personal expression, and quality in writing workshop, taking pains to explicitly deny that their images and artifacts had verbal meanings ("just a design") or held potential as a final product ("just for practice"). These denials allowed them to operate under the radar, to play around with action modes during writing times, and to create meaningful nonverbal texts and paper technology on their own.

The boys' dodging of accountability and personal expression discourses was supported by other educational discourses. Abbie's developmentally appropriate practice drew upon discourses of child agency and teacher nurture. In the discourse of child agency, the ideal learner is the unfettered male child learning at play and communing with nature (Rousseau, 1762/1979); education is positioned as the foil—as artificial, feminized, and passive work assigned by the teacher as Other (Burman, 1994; Cannella, 1997). Literacy, particularly reading, is the epitome of passivity in this view. The "boy problem" draws upon this discourse to construct a struggle against feminized classroom spaces where playing and drawing with popular media (e.g., playing video games, drawing comic books) are suppressed and not recognized as proper literacy practices (Newkirk, 2006, 2007; Ranker, 2006).

In the discourse of teacher nurture, children are developing and unknowing innocents who need physical activity and opportunities to play, under the watchful protection of (female) teachers (Grumet, 1988). An overriding directive to nurture prohibits forceful oversight or disciplinary action. Instead, teachers are to control activities through indirect suggestions rather than commands, in ways that mask their power as adults and, in some cases, allow children to ignore their suggestions.

The overwhelming presence of nurture discourse in developmentally appropriate practice combined with interpretations of literacy as gendered activity more appropriate for girls makes it difficult to perform "boy" *and* "reader" in some early childhood classrooms (Nichols, 2002; Solsken, 1993). Some literacy scholars recommend making "a bigger room" (Newkirk, 2002) for "boy-friendly" (Fletcher, 2006) forms of writing: video game genres and topics, cartooning, gruesome storylines, and gross humor. In a classroom that exuded feminine nurturing, amplified by the Abbie Wannabes, Just Guys were able to do just that: make a place to express masculinity and cordon it off from teacher (feminine) intrusion by framing it as "just drawing." At the same time, due to Abbie's expanded view of literacy, they were able to be recognized as "good students" and to get their drawings and constructions valued as meaningful expression.

In part, this recognition supported and was supported by play and design practices and action modes that fit well into a trans-discursive emphasis on playful child-directed exploration, legitimating the boys' production of a learner-centered space for peer mediation as well as exploration of materials. As noted in the previous chapter, schooling discourses can restrict play opportunities for young girls, imposing identity expectations for cooperation and passivity when girls are interpreted as teacher helpers who work quietly with verbal modes and print media while boys are interpreted as active explorers who need to play to learn with action modes and hands-on materials (Newkirk, 2002).

Masculinities

Masculinities and femininities are multiple and situational, not fixed or binary. On the playground, more variation in play practices and preferences is apparent within each gender category than in cross-gender comparisons (Thorne, 1993). Gender expectations conflate with social class and ethnicity so there is no unified discourse of masculinity or femininity. One version of a *hegemonic masculinity* (Blaise, 2005b; Connolly, 2004) circulates among working-class boys as the need to display and compare physical strength while a middle-class variant of this dominant masculinity values displays of skill, particularly with technologies (Connolly, 2004).The boys' competitive activity, productive work, and cooperative projects aligned with discourses of hegemonic masculinity in sports fandom (Crawford, 2004). Their production of visible work and claims of original ideas reproduced a hegemonic masculinity that supported their competitions and reinforced their boys-only boundary (Blaise, 2005b). Gendered expectations in these discourses determined who could be considered an "appropriate" sports fan and excluded Lin, even though she shared the boys' avid interest in university sports. Just Guys' talk, design, and play about Midwestern University in particular and about sports in general reflected a grammar-irreverent discourse articulated nationally by television sportscasters and statewide by Eagle boosters ("How 'bout them Birds?"), directed to a predominantly White male working-class audience.

> Sport is without question a significant element in the construction of gendered identities. Despite its highly visible presence as an element of popular culture, it is also the element that is most clearly gendered. Men are expected to be interested in sport, women are not. . . . Sport confers and confirms masculinity; an interest in sport problematises femininity. . . . [Sport is a] "cultural field that is, in part precisely about notions of maleness." (Whannel, 2001, p. 10)

> The very processes of construction of sporting heroism have involved exclusion, hierarchisation, marginalisation, and symbolic annihilation. The modes of address employed in sporting discourse most characteristically address a male heterosexual and implicitly white audience. Yet there is also always an attempted inclusiveness—an attempt to construct imaginary coherence of sports fandom and national identity that embraces female as well as male, black as well as white (but not gay as well as straight). Indeed the commercial imperatives of sales and ratings require constant attempts to pull in the marginalized. (Whannel, 2001, p. 12)

Just Guys fit the tacit all-White male demographic for sports fandom and displayed their affiliation with sports teams through their consumption of sports products: clothing with player's names, school supplies with team logos, and references to sporting events they had attended or planned to attend.

> being a [sports] fan most often (and increasingly) is associated with consuming: be that attending a "live" sport event, watching it on television, buying a team's replica jersey, observing the displays and performances of other fans, or any other multitude of fan related consumer practices. (Crawford, 2004, p. 34)

MEDIATING FOR INCLUSIVE PLAY SPACES

The recognition of the exclusionary nature of Just Guys' play and the potential long-term economic effects of children's play interests and literacy choices calls for a more nuanced understanding about the interaction of gender, literacy, and play.

> [D]espite girls' development of more sophisticated literacy skills than boys, in the world beyond the classroom greater value is placed on the kinds of literacies developed by boys. Kanaris [1999] specifically links her argument to the world of work, arguing that girls' efforts at perfecting literacy skills, such as narrative writing, is insufficiently valued in workplaces, compared to the higher value placed on the kinds of literacy skills (with relation to technology use, for example) developed by boys, through which masculinities are secured, rather than threatened. (Davies & Saltmarsh, 2007, p. 17)

This "long view" of boys' designing as preparation for a capitalist workplace contradicts popular constructions of a "boy problem" that presents boys as at-risk due to an overly feminized early education and literacy instruction. Instead, it values design and technology interests and positions girls as disadvantaged by their early compliance and good worker identities.

This positioning has implications for how we interpret children's literacy practices at school. Rather than attributing some innate propensity to either sex that gets constructed as a boy problem or a girl problem, we need to ensure that all children have access to the literacies—print, embodied, and playful design—that are needed for future success.

Providing play opportunities is clearly not enough to ensure equitable learning. Teachers need to be critical readers of children's play so that we can engage groups effectively. Abbie did this effectively by recruiting families' expertise and tapping into children's areas of cultural knowledge as resources for classroom learning. She was able to interrupt exclusionary tactics by mediating rather than taking a "hands-off" stance on children's play and learning. Her approach merged and capitalized on peer culture and school culture values in ways that maintained the integrity of both. She could actively build a bridge into the boys' group because she knew what they valued, a bridge that was built with literacy resources: books on origami and a play center for teaching paper folding. Abbie's mediation placed Lin in the role of master designer and allowed her to wield the skills she already had and to be recognized in the group.

We need to resist the equally erroneous beliefs that children's play is innocent and all-good or that literacy is all-powerful and cures all ills, the "literacy as snake oil" fallacy (Larson, 2007). Rather, we can recognize play as a powerful literacy that creates social spaces rich with opportunities and rife with pitfalls. Better understanding of the boundary work in children's play can help teachers break down exclusionary practices tempered by the recognition that literacies alone, no matter how transformative, have insufficient power to overcome large-scale systemic inequities.

CHAPTER FOUR

Boys and Girls Playing Disney Princesses and (Re)Writing Gender

At the kindergarten writing table, Niko picks up a palm-sized rectangular mirror, breathes onto its shiny surface, and traces a finger in the fog, making small squiggles. Wiping the mirror clean, he checks his reflection: yellow shirt, large brown eyes, a freckled nose, and cropped dark brown hair. He picks up a purple marker and draws a round face, adding hair in long wavy lines. The table hums with the chatter of five children also drawing self-portraits for "Who Am I?" riddle books. The children fill page after page with picture clues to their identities. Flipping to a fresh page, Niko decides to draw one of his favorite things: Ursula the Sea Witch octopus, a character from Disney's animated film *The Little Mermaid*. Turning to Amy next to him, Niko asks, "Did you see the new Barbie movie? I don't know what it's called but I saw it. It's about Barbie." Flinging his arms out and pitching his voice higher, Niko enacts a bit of the film, "And one of them says 'We're in a movie!' And then they all scream!" Across the table, Dustin and Matt in matching football jerseys look at each other and grimace.

POPULAR MEDIA TEXTS, PRODUCTIVE CONSUMPTION, AND THE PRINCESS PLAYERS

To inspire Niko and the other kindergartners to draw and write identity clues in their "Who Am I?" books, Abbie encouraged children to write about their favorite toys and media interests. Her permeable curriculum accepted popular culture as an appropriate and important resource for literacy that allowed children to import and incorporate their media favorites into writing workshop activities. However, this permeability also allowed restrictive gender discourses to seep into the classroom along with snippets of dialogue from a Barbie movie, *Little Mermaid* character drawings, and similar popular media texts.

When children play with popular media in early childhood classrooms, gender discourses collide and converge with discourses of capitalism, schooling, and media. A discourse includes widely circulated scripts that, along with its social practices and values, constitute the identity kits necessary for belonging to a global social network, in this case, Disney Princess fandom. Each discourse constructs and explains a particular vision of childhood, legitimating some identities and not others, evident in numerous critical discourse analyses and cultural studies of children's gender play (Blaise, 2005b; Thorne, 1993), children's media and consumer culture (Buckingham, 1997; Marsh, 2005b; Pugh, 2009, Tobin, 2000, 2004), and toys in children's material culture (Goldstein, Buckingham, & Brougère, 2005; Hartmann & Brougère, 2004; Jenkins, 1998; Seiter, 1993). Some media studies (Giroux, 1999; Haas, Bell, & Sell, 1995) critique the hyper-feminine characterizations in Disney Princess storylines that portray girls as beautiful victims. However, critical research in popular culture shows that children do not simply accept gender stereotypes in popular media (Lee, 2008; Marsh, 2005a; Tobin, 2000; Vasquez, 2005). Further, a view of children as passive consumers does not explain how Niko could occupy a position in a discourse so vigorously directed at girls. The notion of convergence offers a way to interpret Niko's drawings of Disney characters and performance of a Barbie movie scene as an act of consumption that is much more than mimicry of media narratives. It's also an act of production as writing and play practices converged to produce a new text when Niko appropriated media content to add to his book and enacted a bit of film to entertain his tablemates.

The earlier chapters show that children's take-up of gender discourses can position them as girls and boys in ways that influence their peer relationships or interfere with equitable opportunities to learn. As illustrated in the response to Niko's Barbie performance, children who blur gender categories can face sanction from their peers. Matt and Dustin shared a look that produced layered social effects: silent disapproval that created a bond and a boundary. These Just Guys enacted dominant masculinity and sports discourses as they reacted together by making faces at Niko's portrayal of a doll marketed explicitly to girls. Their matching clothing and joint action affirmed their membership in American football fandom and simultaneously positioned Niko's performance as an aberrant masculinity.

We also need to know more about the consumer texts conveyed through the dawn-to-dusk barrage of commercial messages in modern childhoods and the complicated ways that children take up and resist identity expectations circulated through popular media. The tensions among the multiple discourses surrounding princess play in Abbie's classroom raise the question: How does making room for play with popular media during writing workshop bring in stereotypes and open spaces where children can uphold, contest, or blur masculinities and femininities? This chapter provides a glimpse into the interplay of femininities and masculinities when boys and girls play in and out of the desires and confines of passive princess roles and female consumer identities in Disney Princess media.

Two boys, Niko and his brother Peter, and three girls, Zoe, Clare, and Mei Yu, made up the Princess Players, a play group who regularly replayed Disney narratives in their doll play in the dollhouse and eventually wrote books and plays about Disney Princess characters. All the children in this group had transnational backgrounds with family members in other countries: China (Zoe, Mei Yu), the Philippines (Clare), and Russia (Peter, Niko). The Princess Players spoke English at school but said that they could speak another language as well, although Mei Yu was the only one who demonstrated this. The five children experienced tensions in their Disney Princess play that conflicted with family cultural values and contradicted peer gender expectations: For the Chinese-American girls in the group, the characterizations of evil or comical dragons in *Sleeping Beauty* and *Mulan* conflicted with family values and cultural traditions that revered dragons, and for the boys in the group, enthusiastic doll play resulted in teasing from other boys in the class.

In the Abbie Wannabes chapter, nexus analysis showed how the grid of social practices in Abbie's classroom supported a peer apprenticeship, sustained by overlapping discourses of teacher nurture, child agency, and school accountability. In the Just Guys chapter, multimodal analysis showed how multiple modes interacted during peer mediation and competition to produce a boys-only social space, enabled by sports discourse and a hegemonic discourse of masculinity despite conflicting discourses of schooling. In these chapters, the interplay of global discourses was examined indirectly: through practice-first perspective on Abbie Wannabes' play and reading activity and through mode-first perspective on Just Guys' play and design activity. This chapter examines the Princess Players' literacy play through a discourse-first perspective. In this chapter, critical discourse analysis (Rogers, 2011) focuses on the interplay of global discourses to understand how Niko and other Princess Players enforced and contested prevailing gender stereotypes as they played with dolls and wrote popular media texts (see Appendix D for an explanation and extended example of critical discourse analysis). In their plays and books about Disney Princess characters, the children used the convergence of media, gender, and school literacy discourses to portray identities as girls and boys, authors and animators, and actors and directors. As Princess Players replayed the familiar film narratives, they rewrote plots they knew by heart and subtly altered character roles to take up more empowered identity positions than dominant discourses allowed.

Following an overview of discourses and play and writing practices, two events in the playing/writing nexus reveal how children pivoted the meanings of Disney Princess media, dolls, and drawings; revised identity texts; and made discourses available and malleable. Close analysis of one chain of events tracks discursive shifts among identities and texts as Zoe authored, wrote, and animated characters in a re-enactment of *Sleeping Beauty*. Analysis of one scene from Zoe's play reveals how Zoe and the children used improvisation and revision to stretch gendered expectations in the fairy tale's plot action during their enactment of her play. In the final sections, the convergence of discourses of gender and production explains how child consumers' improvisations with popular media blurred gender norms. For this play group, a mix of educational discourses empowered girls and boys to play around restrictive identities and write their way in and out of gender discourses associated with the Disney Princess characters and stories that they loved.

Disney Princess Media and Child Consumers

The Princess Players' complicated relationships to Disney products are best explained not through unilateral media consumption but through cultural convergence (Jenkins, 2006), the blurring of consumption and production within identity work, representation, and mediation that typify daily practices in a world filled with branded merchandise and media networks.

> Childhood cultures are made up of interwoven narratives and commodities that cross TV, toys, fast-food packaging, video games, T-shirts, shoes, bed linen, pencil cases, and lunch boxes (Luke, 1995). Parents find these commodity narratives inexorable, and teachers find their cultural and linguistic messages losing power and relevance as they compete with these global narratives. (New London Group, 1996, para 30)

As consumers, children participate in worldwide media distribution and consumption networks for popular media products: by purchasing licensed merchandise, by playing with dolls and action figures, by wearing branded clothing, by viewing films and video, to name a few. However, through their use of everyday goods in the most ordinary routines, consumers also exercise agency as they take up and make sense of products to produce personal meanings and improvise to make their own strategic uses: a *productive consumption* (de Certeau, 1984). Improvisation offers agentic and creative responses to restrictive identity expectations or dilemmas caused by competing discourses (Holland, Lachicotte, Skinner, & Cain, 1998). To understand the potential for productive consumption in Disney Princess media, it is necessary to situate the brand in the relationship between the Disney corporation and child consumers.

In a global array of children's merchandise and playthings, the Disney Princess franchise stands out. The Disney Princess brand, "the most successful property for Disney Toys," produced $4 billion in global retail sales (Disney Consumer Products, 2010) by bringing together 10 heroines from Walt Disney Pictures' animated film classics: *Snow White*, *Cinderella*, Aurora from *Sleeping Beauty*, Ariel from *The Little Mermaid*, Jasmine from *Aladdin*, Belle from *Beauty and the Beast*, Pocahontas, Mulan, Tiana from *The Princess and the Frog*, and Rapunzel from *Tangled*. Five Disney Princess films are among the six top revenue-generating Disney films of all time. Recent films debuted with blockbuster openings and widely televised movie trailers. After each film's release or rerelease from the Disney "vault," children are able to watch each film—and its direct-to-video spin-offs—again and again on DVD, logging hours of at-home and on-demand viewing. These marketing strategies build breadth and depth in the market, creating widespread and long-lasting demand for Disney Princess films and related products. Daily opportunities for girls to identify with characters in the films and repeated viewings ensure that the princess dolls and sidekick action figures come pre-packaged with familiar storylines that millions of children know by heart.

Young girls, ages 3 to 5 years old, are the target market for Disney Princess multimedia and an accompanying line of licensed toys, collectibles, apparel, and household goods featuring the film characters. The franchise includes a bedazzling collection of pastel products that include animated films, DVDs, toys, music CDs, books, interactive web pages, video games, costumes, clothing, bed linens, school supplies, makeup kits, and even Cinderella dust mops (Iger, 2006; Noon, 2005). Identity messages circulate through merchandise that surrounds young consumers as they dress in, sleep on, bathe in, eat from, and play with commercial goods decorated with popular-culture images, print, and logos, immersing children in products that invite identification with familiar media characters and communicate gendered expectations about what children should buy, how they should play, and who they should be (New London Group, 1996). The pervasive availability of consumer products associated with the Disney Princess films blurs the line between play and reality, allowing children to *live* in-character: One can be Cinderella all day long, sleeping in pink princess sheets, eating from lavender Tupperware with Cinderella decals, and dressing head-to-toe in licensed apparel, from plastic jewel-encrusted tiaras to fuzzy slipper-socks.

Fascination with Disney royalty also travels to school, toted in pink backpacks and lunch boxes decorated with large smiling princess heads. In some classrooms, popular-culture media and toys are relegated to the unofficial space of the playground, deemed inappropriate topics for classroom goals of learning to read and write. However, in classrooms with permeable curricula, children selectively choose material from their popular-culture repertoire for literacy play themes (Dyson, 2003; Marsh, 2003). Abbie's play-friendly permeable curriculum incorporated toys and stories into writing workshop activities, enabling children to replay and rewrite the well-worn storylines and characters from Disney films and to use princess themes to fuel their passions and impress their peers.

Toys as Texts

Toys represent a special kind of child-oriented text specifically designed to enable children to easily recognize the ways they can be used in play (Brougère, 2006). For instance, toys associated with children's popular animated films or television programs encourage children to play and replay familiar scripts and character roles. These media toys are multilayered texts that set literary limits and social boundaries. On one level, Disney Princess toys inspire children to replay remembered plots and recite memorized scripts, providing canned narratives that shape children's play; on another level, the film scripts and characters convey more subtle messages about identity and status that relate to global markets and societal beliefs about gender and childhood (Edmiston, 2008). Toys must communicate meanings that appeal to children in order to be taken up and must be malleable enough to allow players to invent new meanings; that is, toys invite a particular meaning and simultaneously enable its revision (Brougère, 2006). Reconceptualizing play as a literacy requires rethinking toys as 1) texts to be read, performed, and consumed with meanings suggested by their materials and histories of attached storylines and practices and 2) texts to be written, produced, and revised as children improvise new meanings through play.

Dolls as Identity Texts

Dolls and toys also come pre-packaged with discourses and situated identities—*consumer, princess, girly girl*, and so on. Victoria Carrington (2003) analyzed Diva Starz dolls as texts in the context of a "textual landscape" that merges consumer expectations in global markets and gender expectations in popular media. Diva Starz talking dolls communicate a "hip" quality through their materials as well as their prerecorded one-liners and the *z* in the brand name. The dolls' material aspects update a classic Barbie design by adding Japanese anime facial features: nonexistent ears, tiny nose and mouth, and enormous eyes that cover one-third of the face. This *cool girl* identity is strengthened by trendy hairstyles, makeup, and clothing. The doll's snippets of talk, "I'm bored—Let's go shopping," voice gendered consumer identity messages for children in the target demographic, 6- to 12-year-old girls. Carrington's analysis interrogates the popular dolls as *identity texts*, complex texts that require children as readers, players, and consumers to coordinate messages about taste, cultural capital, and social status (Bourdieu, 1986).

It is incumbent upon us, then, to examine the kinds of messages these dolls send to our girl-children as they interact with them. They are clearly not printed texts. Instead, the Divas are powerful markers of the necessary expansion of the notion of "text" in contemporary post-industrial societies and, more specifically, in discussions around literacy. (Carrington, 2003, p. 84)

I suggest that Disney Princess dolls are identity texts that also "talk," not through prerecorded audio clips but through their sedimented film plots, scripts, and songs. Disney Princess dolls index damsel-in-distress narratives with princess victims and princely rescuers, a classic trope in children's literature and play themes that "prepare[s] the ground for the insertion of the little girl into romantic heterosexuality" (Walkerdine, 1984, p. 163). For example, girls are often portrayed as dependent and innocent (with sexual undertones) ingénues waiting for a royal husband as life's fulfillment (do Rozario, 2004).

Disney Princess doll identity texts communicate a clear princess identity and a player identity through their material designs. The Barbie versions circulate a common set of feminine beauty norms, regardless of their individual ethnicity: hourglass-shaped body, glossy hair, long-lashed eyes, and heart-shaped face; hair color and hairstyle are emphasized as the primary distinguishing feature. From their glitter-encrusted plastic tiaras to the hems of their color-coded satin gowns, they are swathed in a seductive aura of wealth, sweetness, and glamour.[1] Although Disney Princess fabric-stuffed dolls represent the same characters, they send a different message. The stuffed dolls have soft fleece skin and yarn hair, materials associated with infant toys that signal innocence and invite cuddling. Still, the colors of the yarn hair, shimmery fabric gowns, and ballet slippers on the fabric dolls make up recognizable signs in a color scheme that symbolizes the Disney Princess characters (see Table 4.1).

PLAY, WRITING, AND IDENTITY TEXTS

Identity texts operate in tension with each other, suggesting that in any classroom space, a complicated interplay of discourses shapes children's interactions. In the Disney Princess play group, identity texts from classroom expectations in writing workshop discourse mingled with identity texts from consumer marketing, character roles, and film scripts in Disney Princess media so that during princess play, children could simultaneously be 6-year-olds, students, peers, girls, consumers, and princess characters among other identities. Two of the discourses in playing/writing nexus are examined in this section: emphasized femininity in Disney Princess media and creative expression in writing workshop.

Playing and Consuming Princess Texts

Femininities

Princess pretense exemplifies the ways that children consume gendered identity texts and take up feminine cultural norms as they play and write fairy tales (Davies, 2003; MacGillivray & Martinez, 1998). The princess ideal is the archetype in a pervasive cultural norm of feminine beauty (Baker-Sperry & Grauerholz, 2003), a kind of gendered talk that Mindy Blaise (2005b) identified in a year-long ethnographic study of gender discourses in a U.S. public school kindergarten. Blaise's critical discourse analysis of play activity showed that children regulated each other's gender performances through talk and actions that demonstrated their ability to adhere to the heterosexual matrix (Butler, 1990) that "regulates gender and gender relations so that heterosexuality becomes the 'normal,' right, and only way to be" (Blaise, 2005b, p. 22). For girls, gendered talk included the following: "*wearing femininity, body movements* [e.g., twirling (hair or skirt), curtseying], *make-up, beauty,* and *fashion talk*" (Blaise, 2005a, p. 85, italics in

Table 4.1. Material Features That Symbolize Disney Princess Characters

Disney Princess character	Dress and dress color	Hair color and hairstyle
Cinderella	Light blue ball gown	Light blonde, topknot bun
Aurora	Pink ball gown	Dark blonde, long, curly
Belle	Yellow ball gown	Brunette, long wavy with topknot
Mulan	Silk gown	Black, long, straight
Jasmine	Aqua top and harem pants	Black, long, wavy
Ariel	Shell bikini top with green fishtail; lavender ball gown	Red, long, wavy
Pocahontas	Tan buckskin tunic and skirt	Black, long, straight
Snow White	Blue bodice with yellow skirt	Black, short, curly

original). During princess play, girls focused on achieving beauty ideals and rejected play scenarios that stretched stereotypical male/female roles. Blaise found princess play to be a prime site for gender performances:

> The value that a small group of girls placed on being beautiful and pretty became evident in the dramatic play area while they were pretending to be princesses. . . . Often, early childhood teachers and parents view children's pretend play as "simply play," failing to recognize how gender is created and re-created in these story lines. As children enact the storylines of princes and princesses, the importance of being pretty and the role it plays in creating femininities and masculinities provide another opportunity for locating the heterosexual matrix in the classroom. (Blaise, 2005b, p. 77)

Emphasized femininity discourse stresses gender differences and legitimates the construction of girls as objects of display and boys as subjects with power (Connell & Messerschmidt, 2005). In this discourse, girls are to look pretty and to defer power to boys, apparent in the abundance of grooming products in the pastel aisles in toy stores.

> One important cultural and ideological reading of the narratives of the toy industry shows the construction and repetition of a "hegemonic masculinity" and its corollary: "emphasized femininity." Two separate, opposite gender roles are created and maintained through such images and narratives of Superman and Barbie which, by being separate and markedly different, work eventually to hold a hierarchy of male power in place. (Hilton, 1996, p. 35)

These gender expectations are repeated across all the Disney films, even in the films with more independent heroines: Belle fends off a macho suitor with her passion for reading but eventually falls for the Beast and becomes mistress of the castle and its singing housewares; Ariel, an inquisitive mermaid who defies a domineering father, becomes demure and silent on land in her prince's world (Lacroix, 2004). A recurrent device in recent Disney Princess films is tension around the princess character's decision (requirement) to marry: She often prefers a bad-boy suitor over her father's choice for her husband (do Rozario, 2004). Regardless of her choice, the princess upholds male patriarchy by serving as the key to the kingdom earned by an active, deserving hero. In this way, emphasized femininity discourse operating through beauty ideals objectifies the princess as the prize.

> The rigid gender roles in *The Little Mermaid* are not isolated instances in Disney's filmic universe; on the contrary, Disney's negative stereotypes about women and girls gain force through the way in which similar messages are circulated and reproduced, in varying degrees, in many of Disney's animated films. (Giroux, 1999, p. 100)

The creation of the Disney Princess brand further amplifies the discourse of emphasized femininity by bringing together the 10 heroines, homogenizing them by highlighting their common beauty ideal and washing out their slight variations in personality and power to control their own destinies. It is a highly effective marketing strategy; millions of young consumers continue to purchase the dolls and play the accompanying princess identity texts, demonstrated by the unflagging global popularity of the brand since its creation in 1999 (Disney Consumer Products, 2010). However, the next example shows that during doll play, boys who played princess characters acted as productive consumers to animate and twist this hyper-feminine discourse in ways that marketers might not have anticipated.

Animating dolls and discourses

> Three boys sit on the floor of the kindergarten room in front of the three-story plastic white, pink, and lavender dollhouse. Niko picks up a blond doll in a red ball gown to enact the evil queen in *Snow White*, "Mirror, mirror on the wall, who's the fairest of them all?" Peter, playing the role of Snow White, bounces a small doll along the carpet and intermittently calls out "Snow White! Snow White!" Adam, who is holding a tiny plastic baby doll, asks, "Do you like to be the lady??" Peter corrects him, "I'm Snow White." A few minutes later, Peter suggests to Niko, "How 'bout we are both fighting? HiYA! HiYA!" The play action immediately transforms from a castle scene to a fight between Adam's baby and Niko's queen as both boys use the dolls to slice the air with karate moves. Finally, Peter reclaims the film's storyline by switching to the role of one of the seven dwarves and restarts the action just after Snow White bites the poison apple: "Oh-Oh! Snow White! Snow White! Snow White! Wake up! Wake up!" Peter and Niko (suddenly also a dwarf) pretend to cry over Snow White.

Although Mei Yu, Clare, and Zoe animated classroom dolls as princesses in family mini-dramas that reproduced the Disney storylines, Niko and Peter preferred to transform Disney heroines into superheroes in wild fantasy episodes with karate fights, flying baby cribs, or demented fairy godmothers. Children animated dolls by moving them and speaking for them, keying their activity as pretense by changing the pitch of their voices and looking directly at the object while speaking (Sawyer, 1997). In addition to the Disney Princess dolls that children brought from home, favorite classroom toys included the "princess doll" (a Barbie's-little-sister-type doll in a long red and pink gown whom Niko animated in this example as the evil queen) and nursery furniture that included a baby swing and two cribs that could be turned into spacecraft or racecars. Dolls, action figures, and stuffed animals are particularly meaning-laden texts that invite identity transformation as children animate the materials and project play identities through them.

Authoring Texts in Writing Workshop

Creative expression

Although children readily collaborated and improvised story meanings as players, they adhered more closely to their own interpretations of familiar storylines when writing books. The emphasis on individual creative expression in writing workshop encouraged talk among children, but not the intensely collaborative talk necessary to sustain shared meanings during dramatic play. This was consistent with creative expression discourse (Ivanič, 2004) that stresses the development of individual "voice" in the production of personal narratives, crafted by authors who primarily work alone albeit informed by writing conferences with teachers and peers. Accordingly, the kindergartners worked on writing projects individually, stopping occasionally to glance at and comment on a neighboring child's writing.

The discourse of creative expression provides a foundation for writing workshop, encouraging learner agency and free expression through a set of routine practices that solicits children's ideas, encourages talk among peers, empowers autonomy in writing decisions during teacher writing conferences, and explicitly refers to children as authors (Newkirk, 2007; Wohlwend, 2009a). This is not to imply that discourse is the same as lived experience; numerous studies have shown that children's writing in school can hardly be called *free* expression as it is monitored and constrained by teacher and peer sanctions (Finders, 1997; Kamler, 1994; Lensmire, 1994). Yet in Abbie's classroom, children exercised a remarkable degree of autonomy. At the beginning of each writing workshop, children told Abbie what they would be working on, not the other way around. During workshop, children abandoned projects on their own (without asking for teacher permission, which would have been superfluous), consulted with other children if they wanted opinions or help, and declined or ignored Abbie's proffered suggestions toward revision when they thought their original idea was better.

Approximating print to write

At the ABC table, Zoe brushes back a strand of silky black hair and uncaps a marker. Peter and Zoe are writing stories about Mulan, the heroine in a Disney animated film set in China. Zoe's story is her own invention, "when Mulan's mom got married." Peter lists characters from the film's sequel, "In Mulan 2, she has three friends and they are the three princesses." He writes the words MoolaNe2! across the bottom of the page, adding an exclamation point because "I am serious."

Through approximated print, children coordinated their intended meanings with their emerging understanding of the print conventions for producing text, usually resulting in a combination of letters and punctuation. Peter's approximation *MoolaNe2* for *Mulan II* demonstrates his coordination of meaning (i.e., the title of the Mulan direct-to-video sequel) with grapho-phonic conventions (e.g., using letters "oo" to represent the phoneme /u/ or remembering the visual configuration of a familiar word *moo*; overgeneralizing the need for an "e" at the end of a word) and punctuation (e.g., capital letter at the beginning of proper names; exclamation point to mark emphasis) (Kress, 1997; Martens, 1996). *Approximating print to write* represents the range of ways in which children can negotiate the tension between their personal inventions and cultural conventions for language (Goodman, 1994). In Abbie's classroom, children's approximated writing reflected their easy access to available resources and models: their personal literacy histories (Whitmore & Goodman, 1995), knowledgeable peers or helpful adults, or printed stories, pictures, and charts all around the classroom.

Authoring books and plays

Mei Yu sits, chin in hands, thinking of what to write on the next page of her puppet show script. Pointing to the third page, she announces, "There's 2 kings, 1 queen, and 1 princess. I finished this all yesterday, the whole page." Large letters fill each page:

LIS GO UPSARS	Let's go upstairs
to See MY GAMA	to see my grandma.
Th WAK	They walk
UPsTARS	upstairs.
the qweN AND KeN WAt!	The queen and king went
INtO the KASL!	into the castle
ANd tuc A NAP.	and took a nap.

As in Peter's example, Mei Yu relied on approximation in order to pro-duce print: She coordinated her intended meaning with grapho-phonic con-ventions (e.g., using the letters "tuc" to represent sounds in the word *took* or remembering the visual configuration of irregularly spelled words *into* and *the*, attempting to meet the need for at least one vowel in each syllable) and punctuation (e.g., spacing between words and arranging words in horizontal lines; overgeneralizing the need for punctuation by placing marks at the end of lines rather than sentences; experimenting with exclamation points and page numbers) (Kress, 1997; Martens, 1996; Owocki & Goodman, 2002). However, children's writing practices reflected not only *how* they approximated conventions to get words on the page but also *why* they wrote. Primarily, children wrote to be recognized as authors. In Abbie's kindergarten, the sedimented writing practices in child-made books "authorized" children by providing a product that served as concrete evidence of authorship, a material artifact with cultural capital in this community of emergent writers. Children knew without asking that a freshly illustrated book placed on the big wooden rocker would generate a chance to sit in the Author's Chair, to read the book to the class, and to be admired and questioned at the close of writing workshop.

Authoring occurred when children told, wrote, drew, and/or dramatized connected texts for child-made books that they read from the Author's Chair or plays that they performed for the class to watch and which Abbie videotaped. Children also used iMovie to edit their films with the assistance of parent volunteers and the library media specialist.[2] Over the following two weeks, Mei Yu would complete two more pages, a set of stick puppet characters and props, a castle backdrop, and a storyboard for her puppet show. Evident in Mei Yu's script and storyboard, the practice of authoring included several subpractices that supported children's production of written texts with appropriate genre features: illustrating, developing characters, organizing plot, and adding dialogue. Children's scripts for plays and puppet shows included narrative descriptions like Mei Yu's, dialogue and lists of characters, and storyboards that planned out each scene. The left-to-right progression of scenes in storyboard panels stressed the linearity of narrative, drawing children's attention to action sequences and moving them beyond initial static displays (e.g., "This is a . . ."). For example, Mei Yu's storyboard planned an action sequence for the four characters in her puppet show: a princess, a queen, and two kings. The king and queen were centered in each scene, facing forward, arms at their sides, static displays that show family relationships rather than action. Mei Yu added action by interspersing the character frames with drawings of stairs to show movement between rooms of the castle and by adding props and dialogue to the family display scenes. The emphasis on display rather than action is often read as an indication of girls' passivity in story construction; however, a discursive reading of Mei Yu's storyboard recognizes the possibility that her emphasis on family relationships was a strategic move that coordinated multiple femininities. Her revision added a same-sex partner that reflected her own family experience as the daughter of two mothers. Although Mei Yu's script included a heterosexual norm—a king and a queen—she stretched this norm by adding another king to the royal family in her puppet set and final puppet performance. Mei Yu's authoring suggests a convergence of a traditional fairy tale text and sociodramatic play that reflected her lived familial experiences.

THE PLAYING/WRITING NEXUS

Writing to Play

> Zoe pulls two fabric dolls out of her backpack and hands Clare one of them: a brown-haired doll in a yellow dress. "You be Belle; I'm Sleeping Beauty," Zoe announces, holding up the blond doll in a pink dress. The girls dance the dolls around the edge of the table. Zoe directs Clare, "They're sisters; this one got adopted," pointing to her own doll. Peter approaches the girls, clutching the small red-gowned doll that is part of the classroom dollhouse collection. He suggests, "And I was the little sister of you both," but Zoe cuts him off with an abrupt "No." Peter pauses, then tries another tack, "Can I hold her?" reaching for Clare's doll. Clare hands over Belle and Peter hands her the little doll in exchange.

Negotiating who can play a princess

The Princess Players enthusiastically took up and animated Disney Princess characters when they brought their own dolls and toys to school. Zoe almost always toted at least one doll in her backpack; the variety was impressive, including vinyl Barbie-style fashion dolls and soft rag-doll versions. On one hand, the children's shared recognition of the princesses' symbolic colors and shared knowledge of the dolls' familiar storylines enabled more stability and durability of meanings so that little setup was needed to get play started and fewer interruptions were needed to talk about the next play move. On the other hand, play also opened an opportunity to alter character identities that came with commercial dolls and to reattach play-inspired ones. New identities could be assigned to dolls by explicitly negotiating the change outside the play frame, such as "They're sisters; this one got adopted" in the exchange between Zoe and Clare.

When children play together, they assign, negotiate, and maintain pretended meanings for objects that are consistent with the imagined setting. At times, these negotiations occur outside the play frame (Bateson, 1955/1972) through language that distinguishes the real activity from the not-real activity through explicit talk that assigns play meanings to props. Children are also highly aware of the material meanings of toys and the ways these meanings shape the plausibility of their play performances (Kress, 1997, 2003b). Thus, one child's proposal that a hard plastic Barbie become the baby sister of a stuffed Cinderella doll caused players to stop playing to negotiate tensions between the dolls' contrasting iconic material qualities and associated indexed identity texts about adults, babies, and siblings that conflict with the pretend identities that the children want to symbolize with the dolls. Such contradictory play meanings spark the negotiations and improvised solutions that characterize children's fantasy play (Sawyer, 1997).

Attempts to alter a princess's identity text triggered negotiations to convince other players to accept the proposed change. Play actions that are consistent with children's agreed-upon text/context sustain players' shared meanings, whereas play actions that are incongruous with imagined characters or contexts challenge or alter the direction of play (Corsaro, 2003). For example, Zoe's suggestion to make the dolls sisters was immediately accepted by Clare and easily incorporated into the girls' play. Zoe deftly detached Sleeping Beauty from the princess's royal family and reestablished a new relationship, smoothing over Clare's potential objections with the adoption ploy. The revision fit into the dolls' identity texts: finding or creating a "good family" is consistent with the goals of emphasized femininity discourse (Walkerdine, 1984) and a goal in the abused stepdaughter to princess-bride storylines in *Cinderella* and *Snow White*. However, Peter's proposition to join the girls' play was quickly rejected even though he had played princess stories with Zoe, Clare, and Mei Yu on other occasions. This suggestion was socially skillful. His proposition to add a little sister used several strategies necessary for successful entry bids in children's play groups (Corsaro, 2003): He offered a specific role for his character rather than a general "Can I play?" request; his proposal to add another sibling fit the girls' established family-play scenario; he also had the appropriate capital as an experienced player in possession of a favorite classroom doll valued by the play group (Fernie, Kantor, & Whaley, 1995).

The possible reasons for Zoe's rejection can be found in layers of the children's play histories, including:
- social—to exclude this particular player from this play episode
- material—to reject this particular doll as not officially or credibly a Disney Princess
- meaning-based—to reject the addition of another character in the co-constructed play scenario
- discursive—to enforce and maintain gender boundaries for doll play. Emphasized femininity discourse, expressed through the dolls' material features, media storylines, and advertising messages,

constructs boys as inappropriate players for the hyper-feminine dolls. Although Zoe was happy to include Niko and Peter in princess play themes with the generic classroom dolls, she excluded both of them from play with the commercial Disney Princess dolls.

Of course, other reasons are possible. Regardless of the reasons, Zoe clearly exercised power over Peter by rejecting his entry bid into play. However, Clare restored Peter's in-group status and included him in the play scenario by trading dolls with him, giving him a pre-approved role. By the end of the year, the potential to exercise power during play was increased when Abbie encouraged the children to write and produce their own plays, which allowed child directors to assign character identities to actors and to animate their peers rather than animating dolls.

Reproducing media texts

As Zoe illustrates a page for her *Mulan* book, Peter watches. After a few minutes, he asks, "How about the three princesses?"

Without looking up, Zoe replies, "There aren't *three* princesses."

"In Mulan 2! She has three friends and they are the three princesses."

Zoe dismisses his suggestion and announces with finality, "I only know *Mulan*." Turning to the last page in her blank book, she quickly sketches out a wedding scene.

As Zoe and Peter demonstrated on this and several other occasions, debates arose over what constituted "real" stories, as children drew distinctions between the original films and the proliferation of Disney-produced direct-to-video sequels and television program spin-offs. Princess Players' discussions about their writings and drawings displayed their princess-film repertoires. Children frequently talked while writing to advise each other and to impose their individual recollections and interpretations of the familiar princess storylines. These conversations provided a way of displaying cultural capital in two forms: 1) as Disney Princess media knowledge that indexed a fan identity and 2) as writing knowledge and creative decision-making that indexed an author identity.

Playing to Write

Animating texts

> During Writers' Workshop, Abbie kneels to listen to
> Niko describe Sleeping Beauty, one of the characters he's
> collected in his writing folder.
>
> *Abbie:* How did you come up with the idea for that
>   character?
> *Niko:* Well, that character—that is Sleeping Beauty, and that
>   [pointing to Figure 4.1] character is kinda mean. Lots of
>   the Sleeping Beauties wanted to be a queen, [changes
>   voice to quavery], a old, old queen. [Speaking in normal
>   voice:] So she wanted to be a old, old queen. So they
>   all got mixed up, uh, into her, so she be's more older,
>   [quavery:], a old, old queen.
> *Abbie:* So she's going to be an old, old queen.
> *Niko:* Yeah, she wanted to be but they made her ever never
>   die.
> *Abbie:* Do they cast a spell to do that? How do they do that?
> *Niko:* They made a spell, she got mixed up, I don't know, I
>   know the spell, well, okay, I can tell you.
>   *[Chanting:]*
>   Whine, oh, howa cawla //
>   nin the awin sawl //
>   so win hawla alla cawla //
>   win the hawla dom.
>   *[Speaking:]*
>   And then they got mixed up and when they said to mix
>   up, when they tried to get in her,
>   *[Chanting:]*
>   hawla cawla mina dawla //
>   so win cawla mawl
>   *[Speaking:]*
>   and they got into her.

Not all of the Princess Players sought to reproduce fairy tales with brave
heroes and damsels-in-distress. Niko's drawings and writings appropriated
familiar Disney characters and transformed them with his own twists: an
ancient Sleeping Beauty, princess clones who do spells and chants, a karate-
fighting evil queen, a super-powered Mary Poppins who blasts around
the rooftops. He jazzed up familiar storylines with improvised characters
and dramatic action during animations in the dollhouse. In this writing

Figure 4.1. Niko's "Kinda Mean" Character

conference, illustration and animation acted as catalysts as well as the means for developing characters and text features. When children animated characters and played their written texts, they were more apt to face the need to improvise and later rethink, revisit, and revise their stories. Attention to animating the characters produced a need for dialogue and, in this case, Niko's improvised nonsense verse[3] In writing workshop, innovations on text such as these were valued over retellings, interpreted in creative expression discourse as signs of learner agency and original composition rather than parroting of a familiar text.

Twisting identity texts

Niko's illustrations of princesses were distortions rather than reproductions, exaggerated to the point of parody. He drew female characters who were much more witch-like than regal in their bright red lipstick and purplish eye shadow. Niko's drawings and accompanying narrations had

a joking quality that acknowledged and resisted the wide-eyed ingenuous-
ness of the Disney heroines and instead emphasized their seductive appeal;
in addition to heavy makeup, he often drew in cleavage for characters in
low-cut gowns as in the "Kinda Mean" character. Niko used caricature
to twist familiar princess characters into comical ones that entertained his
peers as he read from the Author's Chair. Niko's performances of princesses
and exaggerated drawings can be read in conflicting ways: as a blurring of
gender roles, a distortion and critique of the fairy tale storylines that emphasized femininity discourse, as a transgression of a dominant discourse
of hegemonic masculinity in which boys do not play princesses, but also as
an expression of masculinity in which overacting and parody makes clear
that he is only playing and that establishes his play identity as very different
from his real identity. Elizabeth Dutro (2002) found that 5th-grade boys
used exaggeration and humor to emphasize their masculinity and establish
a separation from actor and role when they were required to play female
characters in a skit:

> Both the boys and their classmates used laughter to acknowledge that these
> boys were doing something out of the ordinary. The boys displayed enough
> resistance to show that they took on female personae with some reluctance.
> Their exaggerated voices marked the feminine characters as very different from
> themselves. Finally, posing with muscles flexed reinforced their identification
> with masculinity, even if performed facetiously. (Dutro, 2002, p. 466)

It may be that Niko used exaggeration to distort his performances, to
emphasize the contrast in masculinities and femininities, and to construct
the activity as "not-real" play (Bateson, 1955/1972). However, it is also true
that Niko sought opportunities that allowed him to transgress heterosexual
norms and to access and perform hyper-feminine roles.

IMPROVISATION, REVISION, AND AUTHORITY
IN THE PLAYING/WRITING NEXUS

Linking Improvisation and Revision

Artifacts as anchors and links

In the playing/writing nexus, children's play enhanced writing and writing enhanced play. Doll play prompted authors to add more action and dialogue for characters in scripts and storyboards and more detailed illustrations in books. For example, Mei Yu's play practices developed her writing

when, after running through impromptu rehearsals with her stick puppets at the writing table, she added a storyboard and created a castle backdrop and related props, such as paper cocoa mugs taped to popsicle sticks. Similarly, Mei Yu's writing practices supported her play goals when she read her script, giving meaning to her bouncing hand motions as she manipulated stick puppets. However, in many cases, nexus of writing and playing practices did not occur in the same time and space. Instead, children used toys and their writing artifacts to stabilize meanings and identities (Leander, 2002a) and connect story events across a period of days, enabling more complex narratives.

Figure 4.2 illustrates how play and writing practices linked relative to the Princess Players group (shown as a white dotted oval). The starred points indicate the nexus where practices link and integrate. The nexus of authoring and animating practices illustrates how animation developed a need to attend to writing characters, plot, and dialogue as well as the way that storyboards, scripts, and other writings organized children's plays. Practices connected to each other through anchoring artifacts in chains of writing and

Figure 4.2. Princess Players in Playing/Writing Nexus

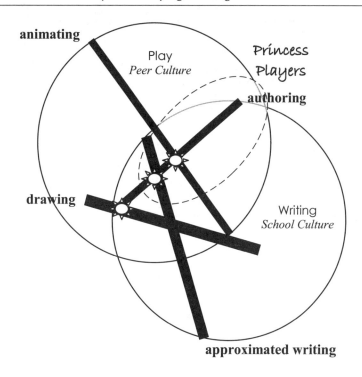

playing events. In these chains, the practice of authoring linked events that involved approximated writing that occurred primarily at the writing table with events that involved animating in the dollhouse or on an impromptu stage.

Dolls and storyboards allowed children to capture their favorite play scenarios by recording in written forms and to access the sedimented meanings and identities that they had previously negotiated with other players. Toys and children's writings held sedimented meanings of commercially produced, well-known Disney identities and storylines as well as the story innovations that children co-constructed during play. Chains of animating and authoring events created and contained transformations of identities and meanings. Dolls, drawings, and writings produced and/or played within these events acted as meaning carriers that allowed children to pick up where they left off as they returned to a project at subsequent times or in different spaces. A child could animate a princess doll one day and, on the next day, find the doll and prop it on the table while recalling the story and drawing a storyboard.

Storyboards provided a crucial link that stabilized story meanings and plot sequences for plays and puppet shows. Children used storyboards as functional tools rather than displays, focusing on their usefulness in planning scenes and directing actors. Zoe sketched out her panels with a cartoonist's speed, allowing stick figures and minimal drawings to communicate the action. She ruthlessly crossed out and wrote over her drawings to correct them. In accountability discourse, her quick drawing could easily be criticized as rushing to be finished or carelessness; in the creative expression discourse in Abbie's classroom, her skillful drafting was appreciated as evidence that Zoe saw writing as a process.

Animating/authoring chains

A chain of writing and play events eventually led to a revision in a book Zoe wrote about *Sleeping Beauty*. In the first event, Zoe used approximated writing to spell and carefully letter the title "SEPN BUDE" on the front cover of her book, adding curling serifs to the letters of the title to simulate Disney Princess commercial fonts. In the second event, the princess-sisters play episode described earlier, Zoe and Clare transformed the Aurora and Belle fabric dolls into sisters and Peter offered his improvised suggestion that his doll join the family as a little sister. Although Zoe rejected Peter's improvisation of a little sister for two princess sisters, she revisited the idea in the third event in the chain when she returned to her book during Writers' Workshop. After drawing a weeping queen and a crumpling princess after Princess Aurora's encounter with a poisoned spinning wheel, Zoe incorporated Peter's improvisation and introduced a new character: Aurora's baby sister appeared in the bottom right corner of the page, crawling toward the action (Figure 4.3).

A much denser chain of events led to transformations during children's playwriting. To produce a play based upon *Sleeping Beauty*, Zoe linked authoring events that enhanced animation (i.e., writing storyboards, creating cast lists of characters) with animating events that enhanced her written texts (i.e., clarifying character roles, inventing dialogue, and organizing the plot sequence while performing the play). During the play, Zoe created and repeatedly revised a four-panel storyboard with 14 scenes. This authoring/animating chain prompted multiple revisions and improvised transformations of the original fairy tale and Zoe's planned text—by Zoe and by other members of the cast. The following description of the play's videotaped production presents an overview of the total action in the play.

Improvising Sleeping Beauty

Zoe, Mei Yu, Clare, Colin, Marshall, Matt, and Emma sit in the hallway just outside the kindergarten room, ready to begin Zoe's version of *Sleeping Beauty*. I volunteered to do

Figure 4.3. A Page from Zoe's *Sleeping Beauty* Book

the videotaping for the final version of the play that Zoe has written and is directing. Zoe and the cast move outdoors to the playground where she directs the actors by shouting out their actions and dialogue. Zoe periodically checks her storyboard for the next direction, occasionally jumbling her planned sequence of scenes.

1. Scene 1, outside the castle: Zoe is playing Princess Aurora and Emma is playing Maleficent, the Disney villain. Zoe shouts, "You're chasing me," and Emma promptly runs after her in a small circle on the grassy area of the playground. Zoe yells, "Cut!"

2. Scene 2, the castle tower (bicycle rack): Zoe runs and stands next to the bicycle rack that represents the castle tower. She shouts to the prince, "Colin! Colin! You're climbing up my hair." She first tilts her head, Rapunzel fashion, to let her hair hang over the metal bars. Then in her animator role as director, Zoe crouches down and pantomimes climbing hand over hand, demonstrating how Colin should climb up the bicycle rack pole.

3. Scene 3, outside the castle (next to the bicycle rack): Zoe reads her storyboard, "The next scene is . . . Okay! Colin, Colin, Matt, and that's all." Matt, playing the dragon, follows Zoe's direction to breathe smoke at her. Colin is confused about his next line and Teresa (an actor who is watching off-camera) tries to prompt him but Zoe rejects her help as interference. Zoe insists that Colin say "Get away!" and when he does, Zoe runs away from him across the playground.

4. Replay of Scene 1: "Okay! Emma, chase me again!" Zoe runs back onto the grass with Emma in pursuit. "Cut!"

The play continues with scenes in which the three fairies cook dinner in their cottage and the king and queen cook dinner in their castle. When Zoe directs Maleficent to cast a sleeping spell that stupefies Princess Aurora by saying, "Emma, come put a magic spell on me," Emma taps Zoe lightly on the top of her head, and Zoe sinks to the ground and lies rigidly on the grass. As an afterthought, she folds her hands across her chest.

Suddenly, Zoe sits up, runs off camera to consult her storyboard and then returns to her prone position. Lifting just her head off the ground, she calls out directions to the prince, who obediently runs over and revives her with a hug.

These quieter scenes are interspersed with frenetic chase scenes and fencing duels in which the princess/director grabs the sword away from the prince to demonstrate the proper way to jab at a fleeing dragon. When the dragon is finally cornered, Princess Aurora tucks one hand in the prince's arm and with the other accepts a bouquet of oozing dandelions spontaneously gathered off camera during the chase scenes by Maleficent and the good fairies. As the couple walks slowly down the sidewalk, Zoe directs the wedding guests to compliment her, "You say, 'What a beautiful dress you have on.'"

At each step in the process from storyboard to video production of the *Sleeping Beauty* play, Zoe wavered between faithful replication of a movie that she loved with its beautiful, archetypically passive princess and creative innovation that offered more active and satisfying feats for her own character. In these improvised transformations, she chased down the dragon while shouting "Surrendah!" and jabbing at the retreating actor with a cardboard sword.

Revising Sleeping Beauty

Zoe's storyboard, shown in Figures 4.4, documents her transformations of the Disney film plot. Repeated revisions removed Scenes 5 and 6 (top half of Panel 2), added a wedding scene at the end (Panel 4), furnished explanatory print (e.g., "The Sleep" in Scene 8 in bottom right corner of Panel 2 and stage directions (e.g., "They hug" in Scene 11 in bottom left corner of Panel 3, and provided actors with interesting dialogue (e.g., "Rock on!" in Scene 10 in the top right corner in Panel 3), including a cryptic sequence between an imprisoned Princess Aurora and the villain Maleficent: "Why?" "Because" (Scene 2 in top right corner of Panel 1). She added long hair to one of the characters in the duel in Scene 7, changing a dueling prince into a dueling princess (Panel 2).

Zoe's struggle with the passivity of the princess in the Disney text is apparent in her storyboard revisions. Except for the final frame with a wedding portrait, Zoe's storyboard is filled with narrative representations that show characters *doing something* rather than conceptual representations of static

Figure 4.4. Zoe's *Sleeping Beauty* Storyboard

Panel 1

Panel 2

Figure 4.4. *(continued)*

Panel 3

Panel 4

displays that show characters *being someone*. In visual analysis (Jewitt & Oyama, 2001; Kress & van Leeuwen, 1996), narrative representations are identified by the presence of vectors, lines—frequently diagonal—that flow between principals and indicate action. In Zoe's initial drawing of the prince and princess in Scene 11 (bottom left frame in storyboard Panel 3 in Figure 4.4), the vector of a single diagonal lip line that connects the two figures' mouths represents a kiss. Vectors are dynamic, indicating that something is happening. Further, vectors are bidirectional so the point of origin must be determined by other information on the page. Of course, the *Sleeping Beauty* storyline explicitly provides this information: The prince is doing the kissing. In fact, the entire fairy tale revolves around the central theme of prince as heroic rescuer and princess as comatose victim, but the point here is that multiple graphic elements of Zoe's drawing cumulatively stress this active/passive relationship. The placement of the prince's head above the princess's head, combined with the diagonal vector of the kiss, which signals motion, visually communicates that the prince is the originator of the action, and the princess is the recipient. The active/passive relationship is expressed in two ways: vertical/horizontal and armed/armless. The primarily vertical orientation of two vectors that are the prince's arms juxtaposed against the horizontal orientation of the armless princess reiterates that he is active and she is passive. In her first revision, Zoe labels this scene "CICC" [kiss]. In the following revision to the panel, she crosses out the word *CICC* and pencils in arms for the princess, which changes the kiss to a hug and makes her character slightly more active through the addition of two princess-originated vectors. She scribbles over the kissing faces and writes "teey Hude" [They hug]. This revision from kiss to hug, which is probably more acceptable in both peer and school cultures, is played out in the rehearsed version and the final videotaped version of her play. Important to the notion of child-made artifacts as layers of sedimented identities, Zoe continued to revise her storyboard to record the changes from passive to active princess, even after the final videotaping.

Negotiating Authority and Pivoting to Improvisation

Plays were particularly rich transformative events that created tiered performances and relationships, allowing author/animators to manage characters indirectly through actors who enacted the characters directly. As an author, Zoe could revise her text to reflect her personal interpretation of the film. As an actor playing a princess, Zoe could interact with the other actors but in ways bounded by her own pre-planned text. As an animator, Zoe could cast and recast actors' roles, critique them, and enforce her expectations for their performances. In contrast to doll play, where animators controlled inanimate objects, plays provided opportunities for actors to challenge the animator's direction.

For authors/animators in Abbie's classroom, plays offered dual opportunities to animate fantasy characters and to direct other children from an authorized leadership position. Zoe, energized by this empowered position, ran around at an almost manic pace during the filming. In contrast, the other actors acted stiffly and stood passively to the side. At first, I was surprised that children who were so lively and inventive during enactments in the housekeeping center were so silent during child-written plays, pantomiming their actions and rarely speaking outside the play frame.

This was demonstrated by Zoe's and Colin's restricted innovation and miscommunication in Scene 3. Colin, a talented and inventive actor with a gift for creating startlingly realistic dialogue, could not envision the passive role for the prince that Zoe intended. Zoe clearly depicted this passivity in Scene 3 on her storyboard (Panel 1 in Figure 4.4). In this frame, the dragon blows steam on a screaming princess while the prince walks away holding sword and shield, his head down and back turned to the action. (See Appendix D for close analysis of 17 turns of interaction during the miscommunication in this scene.) I realized that although the children could improvise and collaborate during their own enactments, they were constrained by authorial expectations when enacting someone else's script.

Table 4.2 lists the scenes and the improvisations and revisions that occurred in a chain packed with transformations, from the creation of the storyboard to the rehearsal, videotaping, and final revision that Zoe made after filming was finished. For example, Zoe repeatedly reworked Scene 7. At the rehearsal, she first switched the action and characters from a sword fight between Maleficent and the prince to a chase scene in which the prince was to jab and chase a fleeing dragon. After the dragon chase resulted in the two actors running wildly in circles, Zoe made some revisions to her storyboard. She added dialogue to the scene and made a sword prop for the prince by taping a paper triangle to a cardboard wrapping paper tube. These revisions successfully provided more structure for the scene when it was replayed the next day for the final performance. However, Zoe was not satisfied with the prince's fencing style of wagging the sword at the dragon. Zoe rushed into the action, calling out, "Do it like this, Colin!" Taking the sword from him, she held it out stiffly and alternately lunged and galloped after the dragon until she backed him against a wall. Finally, even though videotaping was finished, Zoe recorded a final change on her storyboard by adding long hair to the prince's head and changing the prince to a princess (Scene 7 in Panel 2 in Figure 4.4). This transformation dramatically illustrated Zoe's ability to direct and to rewrite the role of helpless victim.

Table 4.2. Play Improvisations and Storyboard Revisions by Scenes

Scene	Storyboard Authoring Planned Scenes	Rehearsals Animating Improvisation	Storyboard Authoring Revision	Performance Animating Improvisation	Storyboard Authoring Revision
1	Bad Fairy chases Sleeping Beauty		Dialogue added		
2	Sleeping Beauty (Rapunzel) in tower		Dialogue added		
3	Dragon attacks Sleeping Beauty		Dialogue added Get Away!	Prince confused; Zoe decides to replay Scene 1	
4	Prince & Bad Fairy fence	Actors chase each other	Dialogue added		
5	Good guy	Actor won't play	Character label added Scene deleted		
6	Fairies make dinner while Princess naps	Actors busy and don't want to play; scene deleted	Scene deleted; Sleeping Beauty's nap moved to Scene 9	Dinner scene added back in; Zoe plays fourth fairy to lead actors	

Table 4.2. (continued)

7	Prince & Bad Fairy fence Prince & Dragon chase each other	Dialogue added; makes sword as prop	Zoe directs Prince, fights Dragon herself, chains Dragon to wall	Hair added, changing Prince to Princess
8	Bad Fairy puts spell on Sleeping Beauty	Caption/Stage direction added: "The Sleep" zzzz		
9	Princess sleeps	Sleeping scene added in	Awakens to check storyboard and direct Prince	
10	Dragon killed; Prince cheers			Dialogue added; Dragon revived
11	Prince kisses Princess	Kiss changed to hug; stage direction added	Dragon chained up by Zoe, forced to attend wedding	
12	The End	Moved after wedding		
13	Wedding	Scene added		Dialogue added
14	The End			

From Disney Princess to superhero

Through the remainder of the school year, Zoe continued to write about and play with the princess dolls she loved but with stronger and more active identities. By the end of the school year, Zoe had transformed Mulan from a Disney Princess to a superhero, improvising an outfit with a short skirt and cape appropriated from her Barbie's wardrobe. Zoe described her doll as follows:

> She's really a princess, but I'm pretending she's
> a superhero. Her powers make her fly. She can make
> tornadoes. She can use power from her hands to make fire.
> Sometimes she makes the bad guy dead with her fire. This
> is how they make her weak: They make a stronger power—
> wind—and they blow her over to the door. My mom got her
> for me when I got back home from Disney World. That's not
> her natural clothes; her natural clothes—but I got this—
> this is my other Barbie's thing—this is her—my Barbie's
> cheerleading skirt. . . . I want her to talk in there. [Lowering
> pitch of her voice and bending close to the digital voice
> recorder.] I have superpowers and I am a superhero and I
> can't have a lot of powers and I can make tornadoes.

In revising Mulan, Zoe materialized her history of practices and identities with the changes to the doll. Zoe's superpowered Mulan differed sharply from the character drawings in the *Mulan* book she had written months ago. Although the Disney storyline (and, of course, the historical text) already enabled a warrior role for Princess Mulan, Zoe had not drawn or written about battles in her book. Instead, the *Mulan* book contained a collection of static displays that looked more like a family or wedding album than a narrative with an active heroine.

Zoe's animation of the doll—"I have superpowers and I am a superhero and I can't have a lot of powers and I can make tornadoes"—voiced her continuing struggle with the tension between active animator and feminine passivity. She transformed a princess into a strong, but still not too powerful, superhero who "can't have a lot of powers." To replace Princess Mulan's "natural clothes" (a traditional silk robe that came with the doll), Zoe appropriated clothes from her "other Barbie's" wardrobe: a short "cheerleading skirt" and a long red jacket. The design of this invented outfit simulated a comic book hero's tight-fitting uniform and cape, which Zoe made more credible when she animated Super-Mulan by holding the doll horizontally and flying it around the classroom.

A follow-up interview with Zoe's mother verified Zoe's interest in su-perheroes and comics at home, confirming that Zoe read "boy comics and all kinds of comics," "loved *Star Wars*," and wrote about superheroes in addition to playing with Disney Princess dolls. Zoe's mother, who grew up in China, hoped Zoe would learn to speak some Mandarin and to write Chinese characters correctly. Because of the film's connection to China, she had given Zoe the Mulan doll and had watched the video with her but was concerned about Disney's portrayals of dragons and Chinese culture as well as other cross-cultural differences between school discourses and her fam-ily's values, such as whether children showed enough respect for teachers and working rather than playing at school.

Transforming the doll from princess to superhero allowed Zoe to ani-mate a more powerful proxy who could fight a bad guy with her bare hands and make tornadoes. The addition of a tornado-making superpower reso-nated with a prominent theme in the housekeeping corner where children played out their personal experiences with a violent tornado that had hap-pened in the community that spring. Peeling away the sedimented identi-ties layered in this doll's revised text reveals Zoe as an active author and animator, as a fashion doll consumer, as a comic book superhero fan, as the daughter of a Chinese mother, and as a tornado survivor.

Artifacts as pivots and markers of authority

The storylines of princess dolls were well known to multiple players and readily available with minimal explanation, enabling the dolls' quick pivots from the here-and-now to fantasy scenarios. These pivots created new texts with familiar character identities while transforming children into produc-tive authors and directors. As Princess Players wrote narratives in books, drew storyboard images, and voiced scripts, their intense focus on meaning-making contrasted sharply with the repetitive labeling of static images (e.g., "This is . . ." or "I like . . .") that was more typical of children's writing in other kindergarten classrooms I observed.

Play transformations had durable effects beyond temporary play scenar-ios. Children's social standing was affected by the identity texts sedimented into the toys they held. When a play group valued a particular object, it be-came prized in peer culture (Kantor & Fernie, 2003) so that an ordinary toy, book, or storyboard was transformed into material cultural capital with po-tential for changing power relations. Among Princess Players, authority to direct play scenarios was influenced by whoever held the most valued dolls: As doll owner, Zoe had the power to distribute the Disney Princess dolls and to act as the leader of play with the right to exclude Peter. However, once Clare actually held the Belle doll, she disrupted these power relations and opened up access to the play group by trading dolls and including him.

Storyboards emerged in authoring/animating chains as key artifacts that concretized authority to direct as well as particular version of the text. Directors positioned actors through physical gestures, acting directions, and repeated references to their own storyboards, albeit with familiar plots and cultural models ("someday my prince will come") and situated identities (e.g., helpless/hapless ingénue as problem, rescuing prince as solution). The storyboard legitimated author/animator revisions to character actions while restricting actor improvisations in ways that influenced the level and quality of each child's participation. However, neither the storyboards nor the performances were finalized (Bakhtin, 1981).

Animation inspired improvisation while authoring encouraged revision through cycles of playing, critiquing, replaying, and rewriting. As director, Zoe had the power to improvise: She replayed a scene to reestablish her intended meaning when Colin misinterpreted her direction to say "Get away!"; she stepped in as a fourth fairy to lead the scene from within the play frame; and she seized the sword to fight off the dragon herself. Repeatedly playing the damsel-in-distress allowed Zoe to experience dissatisfaction as a passive victim and to improvise a more empowered alternative role: After rehearsing and revising the play several times, Zoe first modeled the proper fencing style as director but then decided to keep the sword and fight the dragon herself. Her final revision, drawing long hair on the dueling prince, cemented the transformation of hero to heroine, from prince to princess.

PRODUCTIVE CONSUMPTION AND GENDER DISCOURSES

Girls Making Do and Making Over

The improvisation and revision cycles in Disney Princess play show that children need time to play out and face the limitations of stereotypical gender roles as well as opportunities to act out alternatives. Play allows children to experience dissonance as they enact restrictive stereotypical roles and they must "make do" to find a way to continue to playing. Play also allows children to "make over" that which they dislike, in this case, to improvise to overcome gendered obstacles that blocked more satisfying identity performances. When Zoe performed a princess identity, she experienced firsthand the social limitations of emphasized femininity discourse that constrained her ability to defeat the evil fairy or battle a dragon. Zoe's agentic improvisations align with current research on young girls' play, literacy practices, and popular culture. Anne Haas Dyson's (1989, 1993, 1997, 2003) studies of primary school writing workshop have shown that with teacher-supported opportunities to explore and appropriate popular culture in school, young girls can write their way into positions of more power by authoring roles for peers in classroom plays. Jackie Marsh (2005a) found that when preschool girls played out the stories of *Cinderella* and *Sleeping Beauty*, the "media-related performances of children were not used simply to replicate stereotypical, hegemonic versions of gendered identities, although of course this was a predominant feature. At times, children resisted the normalisation process and presented contested and transgressive models of gendered practices. . . ." (p. 43). However, the subtle and seemingly chaotic transformations in Zoe's animating/authoring show that young girls may already be writing and playing many transgressive texts, revisions, and improvisations that are only visible through close analysis of children's play.

It is important to recognize the range of ways that young girls engage anticipated identities and discourses in Disney Princess merchandise. When Mei Yu, Clare, and Zoe played with and wrote about Disney Princess dolls, they reproduced (and sometimes contested) pervasive gender stereotypes in commercial media and in toy manufacturers' expectations for typical toy-users. Disney Princess dolls and texts provided opportunities to play identity texts associated with discourses of emphasized femininity that the girls found simultaneously appealing and confining. The Princess Players' complicated relationships with princess texts show that the saturation of sedimented emphasized femininity identities in popular-culture toys did not necessarily result in social reproduction of stereotypical roles. There was considerable variation among the girls' animations of dolls. Although all three girls used the dolls to play family themes in castle settings, Zoe engaged and stretched the princess role to accommodate her desire to take charge of her play and direct other actors. Further, boys as well as girls played princess identities and acted out the Disney storylines, although as the example with Peter, Clare, and Zoe showed, boys had a harder time gaining access to the girls' personal Disney Princess dolls.

The Princess Players were avid Disney Princess fans, but they were not passive consumers. Zoe transformed Princess Aurora from victim to self-rescuer. All three girls adapted princess dolls to play out family scenarios that fit into their own experiences, writing a script in which the king and queen go inside the castle to take a nap, turning a princess into an adopted daughter, or drawing weddings to end their books. Play adds another layer to productive consumption when children transact with sedimented identities and meanings in toys. Objects represent but do not exclusively contain a symbolic meaning (Scollon, 2001b). If a desired toy is not at hand, children easily pretend with some other object and reassign the transferred meaning. Manufacturers like Disney can make an expected use for a doll more likely by making it more appealing to a wide audience (popular pastel colors, silky hair, glistening fabrics), but individuals still animate the characters according to their own purposes. When interpreted as productive consumption, such small distortions by consumers constitute microtactics (Foucault, 1978) of everyday creativity that sap the strength of institutions and generate new trajectories (de Certeau, 1984). The Princess Players demonstrate that it is necessary to look closely to see the subtle transactions with identities and text in children's interaction with popular media. The scope of Zoe's productive consumption of a Disney Princess identity and ensuing meaning negotiations with other players was only visible through microanalysis of texts and practices.

Productive consumption is located in a tension between agency and subjection; children are neither cultural dupes at the mercy of global corporations nor cultural geniuses who shrewdly access and expertly manipulate vast networks of gendered multimedia for their own purposes. Although Zoe exercised more agency than the *Sleeping Beauty* storyline actually provided, she still maintained masculine/feminine hierarchical relationships by excluding Peter from doll play, by using princess dolls to write and play family-focused stories, and by culminating her books and plays with weddings for happily-ever-after endings. The global distribution of Disney Princess products means that millions of young girls engage with the same toys and anticipated identities in myriad ways, reproducing and exploring, perhaps even improvising and revising, identity texts that have been regarded as innocent play outside the school curriculum and of little interest to educators.

Boys Making Gender Trouble

Gender is a social construction that does not reflect the complexity of lived lives. Emphasis on gender differences can exacerbate inequitable literacy practices when girls are constructed as passive literacy learners who read and write about school-appropriate topics and boys are constructed as active learners who need special encouragement to engage in literacy (Davies & Saltmarsh, 2007; Nichols, 2002). Concerns about the effects of a purportedly overly feminized education for young boys (Sumsion, 2005) and the related "boy problem" (Martino, 2004) are based on an assumption that schooling for girls and boys should differ according to two largely discrete, homogenous sets of gender-based interests and educational needs. Boys' interests are characterized as out-of-school forms prevalent in popular culture such as science fiction, superheroes, horror genres, and video games (Fletcher, 2006; Smith & Wilhelm, 2002). Girls' interests are characterized as already aligning with school culture, implying that no special attention is needed to integrate or mediate popular-culture material that appeals to girls (Millard, 2003). The notion that boys require special attention is predicated upon beliefs that girls prefer play and writing themes (e.g., doll play, home and family) that are more acceptable to teachers and already align well with school curricula but that special efforts are needed to meet boys' (presumed) need for adventure (e.g., rough-and-tumble play, violent video games). Interestingly, an international study of children's actual toy preferences show that kindergarten teachers are already more apt to provide boys' preferred toys (construction toys such as LEGOs) than girls' favorites (adult fashion dolls such as Barbie) (Hartmann & Brougère, 2004).

This case provides a counterexample. The boys in this play group were passionately interested in doll play and Disney Princess media. Peter and Niko were recognized by their teacher and peers as prolific kindergarten writers who drew female characters and animated their drawings as they wrote daily at the writing table. These drawings accrued further cultural capital in school and peer cultures as the boys shared drawings in the Author's Chair where their storytelling and animation of drawings entertained peers. Niko and Peter regularly shared their drawings at the close of writing workshop, excitedly retelling stories and re-animating the characters in their drawings as they sat in the wooden rocker that served as the Author's Chair. Following these sharing sessions, each boy would call on other children in the audience who raised their hands to offer comments and admiring remarks (e.g., "I like your drawing"). Niko's and Peter's drawing and storytelling abilities, supported by their media knowledge, provided a way to take up successful student identities in school literacy discourse.

The playing/writing nexus allowed Niko and Peter to make "gender trouble" (Butler, 1990), to blur binary gender expectations and disrupt the notion that gender identities are fixed or unified (Foucault, 1978). The merger of media play and writing workshop provided a daily space for Peter and Niko to express Disney Princess fan identities and to present themselves as female characters, made explicit in Peter's self-portrait in which he declares "Peter is a girl!" While Peter preferred to write, draw, and play stories about Mulan and Ariel, Niko wrote about a range of female characters in addition to Disney Princesses, including a book about Mary Poppins, drawings of Bratz dolls, and a play about Catwoman with storyboard and script. Through their princess play and writing, the boys took on multiple, often contradictory, gender identities, in relation to surrounding discourses and in response to positioning by others (Davies, 2003).

> Literacy educators can work to "counter the violence" the [gender] dichotomies provoke in two ways, each of which relies on the other: We must foster multiple and variable performances of gender and sexuality while creating, indeed insisting on, a context where such performances do not come with violent consequences. Making gender trouble in educational contexts demands both of these efforts simultaneously. (Blackburn, 2005, p. 413)

The playing/writing nexus opened space for gender trouble by welcoming story worlds where boys could play princesses in relatively safe play spaces and challenge anticipated identities for girls-only characters and players.

The playing/writing nexus, sustained through plentiful play opportunities during writing workshop, expanded the classroom place, making a bigger room for a range of popular-culture interests and more diverse performances of masculinities and femininities within this kindergarten.

TEACHING FOR CRITICAL ENGAGEMENT WITH POPULAR MEDIA

Permeable curricula heighten the need for critical readings of gender messages in children's identity texts across forms, whether commercially manufactured texts in media toys, embodied texts in play roles, or written texts published through writing workshop. When children choose their own topics for writing, the majority of children's stories celebrate gender stereotypes and these are the books that are read from the Author's Chair:

> Stereotypical children's texts—often more violently and blatantly stereotyped than commercially produced texts—are frequently authorised as classroom reading material. . . . They are "published" and put on display in classrooms so that children can read each other's work, and yet provision to discuss such texts—in terms of what the stereotypes indicate about the adoption of gendered subject positions—seems seldom to have been made. (Gilbert, 1992; electronic version)

There will always be a tension over who holds the responsibility for in-class expression; children pursue their interests to the extent that the teacher fosters them, always shaping what is possible within the classroom (Kamler, 1999; Newkirk & McClure, 1992). When popular media are allowed in classrooms, their associated discourses are not equally powerful or equally tolerated by teachers. Teachers are also subject to gendering, "subject to powerful discursive regimes mobilized by totems such as Barbie dolls or friction trucks brought to school by the children" (Reid, 1999, p. 171). Teachers who act quickly to squelch noisy battles and mock aggression enacted with dueling light sabers may not question the helplessness and demure passivity prompted by princess play or the exclusionary effects of children upholding gender strata with eye-rolling smirks and subtle ignoring.

However, when teachers see the relationships between power, play, and peer culture, they can take more critical stances as mediators. It's important to note that what may at first look like simple mimicry of favorite texts may actually involve more complex manipulations of meanings upon closer inspection. This complexity suggests the need for teachers to study popular media in order to understand how children's favorite films and video games shape peer culture, teaching, and learning in their classrooms. Informed teachers who combine play and popular culture with critical literacy curricula can provide children with guided experiences with popular media and toys that allow them to revise texts that powerfully position them as players, writers, and peers (Vasquez, 2004).

Given the extent of children's immersion in popular media, it is indefensible to relegate popular culture to out-of-school settings. Instead, we need to develop and implement critical media literacy curricula in early childhood and elementary classrooms. Further, critical literacy curricula should be play-based and productive, with opportunities for writing and filmmaking with popular media toys in ways that acknowledge children's attachments but also make commercially given identity texts malleable and open to renegotiation. In this kindergarten, the playing/writing nexus, supported by active teacher mediation and permeable curriculum, enabled Princess Players to play their passions but also to act critically, to make gender trouble, and to disrupt the power relations through fencing princesses and doe-eyed dolls swathed in pink.

CHAPTER FIVE

Play as a Tactic

In each of the three play groups featured in this book, children integrated play with available school practices, modes, and discourses in ways that allowed them to transform meanings attached to their books, art materials, and favorite media toys. The examples in the preceding chapters illustrate children's reading, writing, design, and play practices as literacies that produce print, visual, artifactual, and embodied texts. The concentration of powerful literacies in the literacy play nexus moved children forward in their apprenticeship in school literacy. When play combined with other literacies, the possibilities for meanings and identities proliferated, resulting in enriched book readings, badges of skill expertise, and improvised character performances.

MORE THAN A LITERACY

Play is not only a set of transformative literacy practices but also a powerful means of shaping children's identities and participation in classrooms. Play allowed children to take up powerful literate identities that expanded their opportunities for classroom participation. As pretend teachers, lead designers, and film directors, children could decide, make, and remake the meanings of texts and artifacts.

Classrooms, Place, and Strategies

Children also used play to transform the classroom *place*, a geographically and institutionally bounded context with physical features, cultural histories, and social roles (de Certeau, 1984) structured by the field of schooling. The physical place of the classroom was planned, built, and maintained by the school district and monitored by local fire marshals, safety inspectors, and state health agencies. The school itself served a larger place, families in the neighborhoods within attendance boundaries determined by a local school board that had been elected by the community at large. In this way, the place of the classroom was materially constituted by nested activity in a network of surrounding institutions (Leander, 2002b):

families, neighborhoods, community, state, nation, multinational corporations, global markets, and so on.

Classroom activity is situated in the tension among discourses that promote the political, social, and economic interests of these layered supporting institutions. This kindergarten class was part of a public school district, funded by local and state governments and subject to district policies, departmental agency regulations, state legislative mandates, and federal oversight. In this kindergarten, the school furniture, books, paper, and other materials were allocated by the school and purchased by local school district. (Like many elementary school teachers, Abbie also purchased a great deal of material for the kindergarten herself, especially for the innovative inquiry curriculum that she designed.) The school district provided a literature-based language arts curriculum—marketed by an educational publishing conglomerate as an effective way to comply with standards set by state agencies and federal policies, standards measured by test scores on commercial instruments that are also designed and marketed by the curriculum publishers (Goodman, Shannon, Goodman, & Rapoport, 2004). Although teachers in Abbie's district varied in how closely they adhered to the teaching manual in the commercial literacy curriculum, many exemplary literacy teachers in this district reported that they felt increasing pressure to follow the basal (Schmidt, 2005). In this school district, as in many public school districts, a foregrounded discourse of accountability and mandatory compliance with school district expectations supported a backgrounded discourse of capitalism and global economic competition. Education faces pressures from governments and businesses to provide a workforce that will maintain the United States' status in the economic race with other nations. An ongoing national concern to stay ahead of the competition in an information-driven global economy has translated into demands for acceleration in schools where children are expected to handle more information faster and earlier. Efficiency, productivity, and work ethic combine in a worldview that goes something like: We can't start too soon with the serious business of learning and, therefore, kindergartners should be working at mastering literacy and numeracy, not playing around with dolls or puppets, especially not popular media or paper airplanes. The pressure for acceleration in schools is compounded by national policies that measure learning by testing isolated skills in individual learners (e.g., NCLB, 2002). Faith in standardized testing and skills-based instruction drives scripted teaching and computer drill software programs as well as no-nonsense task-oriented seatwork.

When "objectives are minutely described (and if tests are high-stakes), they invariably morph into classroom practices. Writing instruction comes to resemble test taking, a prompt-and-rubric approach, tightly timed and lacking in any social interaction" (Newkirk, 2002, p. 186).

In other words, literacy practices become strategies, the means of enforcing prevailing institutional motives within classroom. Places are furnished with strategies, institutional (in this case, school) practices (e.g., schedules, curricula, assessments, teaching techniques, and so on) that help maintain order (de Certeau, 1984). For example, instruction often focuses on how well children can display their knowledge of procedures in literacy practices rather than how well they can actually interpret or craft a message (Bloome, Puro, & Theodorou, 1989; Street & Street, 1991). When literacy procedures are used to evaluate and rank students, they act as strategies that structure the classroom place by reproducing students' relative classroom status. Early literacy practices help keep things in place and reproduce existing social hierarchies when learning to read or write involves important lessons that not only teach children how to embody literacies but also which literacies count and who can and cannot take up literate identities (Luke, 1992).

Tactics, Space, and Play

In contrast to strategies, *tactics* are the innumerable small disruptions that people use to appropriate strategies for their own purposes (de Certeau, 1984). Strategies keep things in place but tactics allow us to "make do" with the available resources by inventing new meanings for time and space in a place. Children were able to use play as a tactic to make and remake the *space*, the social sphere associated with the material place of the classroom. While places are physical and institutionally given, spaces are social and subject to interpretation, appropriation, and re-invention (de Certeau, 1984). When Abbie Wannabes enacted the teacher to read books or charts, they created a new space: a school within a school inside Family Circle. Just Guys created itinerant "boys-only" spots for exploring art materials, drawing sports logos, and constructing paper airplanes. Princess Players created new fantasy worlds as they authored books and plays and animated *Sleeping Beauty* and *Mulan* on impromptu stages around the classroom. In Abbie's classroom, play enabled imaginings that layered neighborhood scenes or fantasy scenarios onto the physical classroom space. Children demonstrated considerable agency in all three play groups as they accessed power ingeniously through affordances supplied by immediate material resources and available discourses for identity performances in each nexus (see Table 5.1). However, it would be misleading to suggest that children (or adults) carefully consider each tactic in terms of its discursive effect or power. People take up tactics in artful and/or innocent ways as they do what seems best at a particular time.

Table 5.1. Connections Among Nexus, Classroom Cultures, and Discourses in Kindergarten

Nexus	Place/Space	Strategies & Tactics	Cultures	Discourses	Institutional Activity System
Reading/Writing	Classroom Place	Strategies: Displaying School Literacy Procedures & Skills on Tests	School Culture	Accountability Individual Production Global Capitalism	School Curriculum: Balanced Reading
Playing/ Reading	Family Circle Teacher-Initiated Play Space	Tactics: Enacting (Teaching) & Approximated Reading	School Culture	Feminine Nurture & Child Need Child Agency	Early Childhood Profession
Playing/ Designing	Boys-Only Team Child-Initiated Play Space	Tactics: Exploring, Drawing & Constructing	Peer Culture, Sports Fandom Popular Culture	Competition Hegemonic Masculinity	Sports Industry
Playing/Writing	Writing Workshop Teacher-Initiated Play Space Fantasy Play Child-Initiated Play Space	Tactics: Authoring & Approximated Writing Animating & Authoring	School Culture Peer Culture Disney Media Fandom	Child Agency Free Expression Consumerism Emphasized Femininity	Writing Pedagogy Toy Industry Media Marketing

THEORIZING PLAY AS A TACTIC

Play allows children to live with a text, to try on the tacit expectations in a favorite media story, and to experience a role's constraints firsthand, in ways that can prompt critical response, improvisation, or revision. In Bourdieu's (1977) theory of practice, literacy is a particularly potent way of accessing positions of power. Literacy practices are markers of success; proficiency with school literacy practices determines grades and placements for students and teachers within the field of schooling. Operating as strategies, literacy practices structure and stabilize schools. Children learn these school-valued ways of regulating bodies and managing objects during literacy training at school (Luke, 1992). They also learn dispositions toward these practices, beliefs that shape how students behave and what they desire.

Practices embody habitus, a self-perpetuating and engrained set of dispositions that tends to reproduce hierarchical relationships of class, gender, and ethnicity. In mismatch theories of literacy acquisition, children take up the literacy practices that reflect the habitus that they absorb in life experiences within their families and communities. But when their habitus and literacy practices differ from those expected at school, children lack the authorized "ways with words" (Heath, 1983) necessary to be recognized as successful and literate at school. Further, because these literacy practices are embodied and tacit, they appear fixed and natural rather than sociocultural. However, Bourdieu also argued that although habitus is engrained, it is not immutable.

Children at play reproduce familiar nexuses of practice when pretending to be adults engaged in typical practices in everyday activities, but play can also be used to resist, disrupt, or reimagine the accustomed ways of doing things (Edmiston, 2008). Used this way, play becomes a tactic that manipulates the constraints in here-and-now reality to make alternative realities possible. Play enables children to create diversions and escapes while remaining in the same physical place. It provides more agency by allowing actors to appropriate and twist the official practices of a place to better fit their immediate purposes. Through play, children explore and expand the cultural practices of their worlds, making do with the available resources and improvising to remake and reimagine the classroom space.

Play as a Tactic in Peer Culture

In the peer culture in this playful classroom, tactics abounded. Meanings and identities were always under construction, open to ongoing negotiation and renegotiation and never finalized: All groups improvised as they grappled with tensions among faithfully interpreting given texts or tools, exploring the multiple meanings attached to materials, balancing new play ideas or players with established play frames, reshaping materials to make them personally accessible and sensible, and convincing the rest of the group to accept these makeovers.

Playing school and wielding books

Abbie Wannabes negotiated the text to construct an understanding of a book's meaning; they also negotiated to convince their pretend students to agree upon an interpretation, while trying to keep the play from breaking down and maintaining their authority within the play frame as pretend teachers and play leaders.

The field of elementary schooling establishes sets of relations between teachers and students, good readers and struggling readers, children and adults. A field is "a network, or a configuration, of objective relations between positions structured by relationships within the field and with other fields" (Bourdieu & Wacquant, 1992, p. 97). Fields are also structured by the trajectories of individuals competing for capital within that field so that children whose habitus aligns neatly with school can access positions with more status in the classroom. According to an apprenticeship model in the field of schooling, proficient readers like Adam should have been the mentors, the peer teachers, the students with legitimacy to teach, to appropriate literacy, and to reinscribe school on the bodies of developing readers such as Emma, Lubna, and Jaeden.

However, play allowed reversals and not just reproductions of power relations. Developing readers used play to mediate the field of schooling as a play context, and in the process, opened up otherwise inaccessible positions. Abbie Wannabes and their pretend students wielded reading practices and books as markers of reading ability and power. Familiar books constituted a key material resource that Abbie Wannabes used to display the habitus necessary to get recognized as readers; these books were artifacts of cultural capital, front-loaded with ready-to-use valued practices previously modeled by Abbie in shared reading sessions.

In the field of education, books matter. Cultural capital produces the most significant differences among positions (Bourdieu & Wacquant, 1992) and in school, reading proficiency provides cultural capital. Reading practices with leveled books establish rankings among students in many classrooms. This portrait of Abbie Wannabes' literacy practices challenges a time-honored view of young children innocently absorbing the early reading skills of book-handling. Rather, it shows children as social agents engaged in book-wielding to assume positions as teachers or power brokers within the field of schooling. Abbie Wannabes show that play is a uniquely transformative force that makes it possible for children to step out of local circumstances into imagined ones, in ways that reshape the habitus of students and enable them to reposition themselves in the field of schooling.

Playing to win: Teamwork and boundary work

Just Guys negotiated the affordances and constraints of tools and materials to craft images and artifacts, and they also competed and collaborated with each other to demonstrate their skill and competence as group members while staking out and maintaining masculine territory within the feminized space of kindergarten. Just Guys worked hard at learning to fold paper airplanes or at drawing super-Eagles because their artifacts and drawings allowed them to participate in group activities. The artifacts that Just Guys constructed—SpongeBob puppets, paper cell phones, paper airplanes—acted as entry vehicles for joining the group as well as a means to display skills and to share insider knowledge (Elgas, Klein, Kantor, & Fernie, 1988). Mediation and sharing of knowledge became boundary work in which it was not enough to possess a paper airplane but also necessary to have made the airplane in order to have it function as cultural capital, as a demonstration of one's skill to earn designer status within the group.

The boys seemed to be constantly competing through their design production ("I made hundreds," "I'm making the best paper airplane ever!"). Competition produced in-group rankings and a social hierarchy as well as group cohesion. As Just Guys shared new knowledge and helped each other operate new tools, they also constructed, maintained, and protected their joint activity and group space. New design projects reinscribed their relative membership status by creating novice positions: The introduction of a new project required other boys in the group to seek assistance from the project designer in order to learn its requisite mediated actions. In this way, image and artifact production produced a space that served as a recursive site for acquiring and displaying design skills while concretizing the design history of the event and the designers' relative status.

The boys embodied *teamwork*, a sports ideal that promotes the interdependency of cooperation and competition: Winners work together. Peer mediation was not only a way to get recognized as an active learner and helpful student; it was clearly a way to cooperate and compete. Marshall could foster a peer's skill development while showing off his superior ability. The notion of teamwork foregrounds ideals of cooperation and high achievement while backgrounding its production of a closed group, a team: an *us/them* relationship that enables rankings within a competitive field.

Just Guys worked together in a team space that boys sustained by wearing similar clothing in university team colors, by engaging in shared practices, and by assessing one another's skill. On the playground, they joined forces to compete against other kindergarten classes to play soccer. In the classroom, they settled for drawing and writing about watching and playing university football or Cubs baseball. On one level, this is the innocent activity of young children who share an affinity for sports and drawing. On another level, the boys' activity contributes to habitus in sports fandom that produces insider relationships in industry. In this view, gendered exclusion creates early disparity that advantages boys and provides a leg up in the acquisition of a taste for sports and models of spectatorship favored by middle-class Americans (Kane, 2003). This suggests that the boys' mediation activity is situated in a much larger closed apprenticeship that scaffolds boys into competitive hierarchies in the fields of sports, schooling, and business.

Playing with gender in popular media

As Princess Players negotiated the commercially given storylines and identities of toys and popular media, they remixed gendered storylines that came with beloved toys to create more agentic possibilities for the characters in their texts and productions. Play and design complemented this learning community's habitus, providing creative and constructive alternatives to the reality of lived experience.

In this classroom, Disney Princess media offered ready-made fantasy worlds, complete with attractive characters, memorable language, and powerful discourses. Gender discourses accompanied the Disney Princess worlds that children imagined into classroom places, sedimented with familiar video storylines into dolls and drawings that acted as pivots to easily bridge fantasy and reality. Disney's anticipated identities for ideal media consumers and doll players layered with local classroom histories of children's pretense scenarios and playwriting.

> The key to understanding the currently emerging relationships between media consumers and producers . . . is their complexity. These relationships are constantly reconfigured in a convergence culture, and at times are both reciprocal and antagonistic. Such liquid relationships are seldom stable, generally temporary, and at the very least unpredictable. (Deuze, 2009, p. 8)

In this malleable play space, Niko and Peter disrupted the habitus fixed in children's histories of girls as doll players and Disney's marketing expectations for girls as princess media consumers, drawing upon the transformational power of play to create new social spaces where they could enact feminine identities and test the limits of masculinity discourses.

Similarly, dolls and storyboards offered concrete repositories that carried and stabilized story meanings but were paradoxically packed with potential for transformation. As children played within the universe of possible identities and contexts for pretense, they took up disparately empowered subject positions within discourses of emphasized femininity and creative expression. Because these identities were relational (e.g., princess/prince, actor/director, character/author, boy/girl), play allowed children to access and exert power over peers that might not otherwise be possible in the classroom. From moment to moment, gender-specific identities in popular media and in school literacy discourses were appropriated, reproduced, imposed, resisted, and revised when children wrote and played about media texts during writing workshop.

Play as a Tactic in School Culture

Abbie's use of play constituted a tactic that dodged the clobbering one-two punch of accountability and capitalism discourses, shielding her kindergarten from encroaching and normalizing discourses. Play provided a means of importing alternate discourses through the production of collectively imagined places. In Abbie's talks to the children about their classroom community, she portrayed the classroom as two "as if worlds" (Holland, Lachicotte, Skinner, & Cain, 1998): She wanted the children to view themselves (in essence, to pretend to be in order to become) members of a caring Family Circle and a community of writers in a workshop. Both places are constituted by pervasive and persuasive educational discourses. Nurturing discourse constituted Family Circle through models of teacher nurture, child innocence, and developmentally appropriate practice while the discourse of individual expression constituted Writers' Workshop through ideals of learner agency, creativity, and free speech.

Imagining Family Circle

Abbie's classroom had few routines that fit the drill and practice model. Through daily interactions in the Family Circle space, Abbie transformed the class into an imagined school family. Routine practices in her classroom considered children's comfort: Children joined a group when they were ready, left to get drinks when they were thirsty, or stretched out on the floor during stories to get more comfortable. Abbie's emphasis on maintaining a loving, peaceful atmosphere and her accommodation of children's physical comfort evidenced a feminized nurturing discourse. In contrast to the rigor rhetoric in accountability discourse that exercises strict control over children's minds and bodies (Boldt, 2001), the discourses of adult nurture and child innocence attend to children's *needs*: the need to play, the need for protection, and the need for activity matched to their developmental stage.

Nurturing teachers do what they believe is best for children. Nonetheless, nurturing discourse positions children as needy and adults as powerful; this was apparent when Lubna played teacher. Her power over other children was emphasized as she directed them, pointed to control their gazes, handed out or removed felt characters from their hands, repositioned their bodies, and patted their hands in a reassuring you-can-do-it way.

Imagining a kindergarten playshop

Although Abbie felt that she must comply with district mandates to use the big books from the commercial literacy curriculum during her daily shared reading sessions, she structured the majority of the morning literacy time to allow children to choose their activities and projects. Abbie ensured that children had frequent opportunities to set their own purposes for writing by creating a kindergarten version of writing workshop. A discourse of creative expression circulates through talk that solicits children's ideas, empowers their writing decisions through peer review and teacher writing conferences, and explicitly refers to children as authors. Writers' Workshop offered a place and a set of routines that enabled children to see themselves as authors and playwrights. By the end of the kindergarten year, the agency and expression discourses were invisibly at work within the routine practices of authoring and approximated writing. Writing workshop establishes an overarching play frame within the classroom space as teachers and children form a literacy apprenticeship in which children work and play at being writers.

> In a sense, the teacher in a primary writing workshop says, "Let's pretend we're writers," and the children assume that subject position with images brokered by the teacher as well as other experienced members of the culture (parents, siblings, Sunday School teachers, people on television). The task is not very determined, which affords child writers the opportunity and need to discover, construct, or figure out the task, finding questions and problems not formulated by adults. (Bomer, 2003, p. 228)

The creative expression discourse foregrounded in writing workshop promotes ideals of individual agency and freedom of speech. The limitations in these ideals stem from assumptions that children's peer interactions are ideologically innocent (Lensmire, 1994) and that a teacher's indirect responsive style is culturally neutral. A discourse of free expression privileges a set of mainstream language and literacy practices that are gendered (Comber & Nichols, 2004; Kamler, 1999; Newkirk, 2002), schooled (Cazden, 1988; Mehan, 1979), culturally restrictive (Bloome, Katz, Solsken, Willet, & Wilson-Keenan, 2000; Christian & Bloome, 2004; Heath, 1983), and ideologically marked (Gee, 2001; Lensmire, 1994; Solsken, 1993). Tobin (1995) suggests that free expression is a misnomer; what teachers actually allow is limited to speech and writing that they deem appropriate for school. Of course, teachers who are cognizant of the relationships between power, play, and peer culture may, as Abbie did, take more active roles and critical stances as mediators and teacher-researchers. Teachers who actively learn about their students' peer and family cultures gain critical understanding that enables them to mediate effectively and create equitable learning environments for writing (Gutiérrez & Rogoff, 2003). Writers' Workshop created a place, an "as if" world (Holland, Lachicotte, Skinner, & Cain, 1998) and an inclusive space through Abbie's reframing of this familiar classroom activity.

Abbie's version of writing workshop was child-directed and open-ended, pretended and unpredictable, a *playshop* rather than a workshop, made daily with the children. By recontextualizing the classroom through collective imagining of a nurturing family of writers, Abbie appropriated behemoth educational discourses to reimagine the institutional place and create a livable, supportive space. Table 5.1 maps the overlapping places and spaces, strategies and tactics, and discourses in this kindergarten. The discord among accountability, nurturing, creative expression, and gender discourses produce double binds that appear irreconcilable (Wohlwend, 2009a). As teachers, we often strive to teach within a harmonious and integrated set of discourses that merge practices that are consistent with one another. However, Leander (2002b) argues that conflicts between activity systems often produce opportunities for identity expansion and learning potential. Sites with multiple activity systems produce expanded social spaces as the conflicts between layered contexts produce spaces that are prime sites for learning and identity work. Duckworth (1996) argues for "keeping it messy"—that open-ended learning situations allow wide-ranging exploration that creates more entry points into the learning situation and accommodates a broader range of learners.

JUSTIFYING PLAY

Figures 5.1 and 5.2 illustrate the difference between a classroom like Abbie's that is rich in nexus of literacies (Figure 5.1) and a classroom that sharply separates play and design from other literacy activity (Figure 5.2). Figure 5.2 illustrates the loss of these productive sites for learning and participation when 1) play is completely separated from reading and writing (e.g., children play only at recess or during breaks) and 2) design is marginally included as a supplement or incentive for literacy tasks (e.g., children draw only to illustrate books or construct only to correctly follow directions

Figure 5.1. Nexus of Literacy, Play, and Design Practices in an Early Literacy Apprenticeship

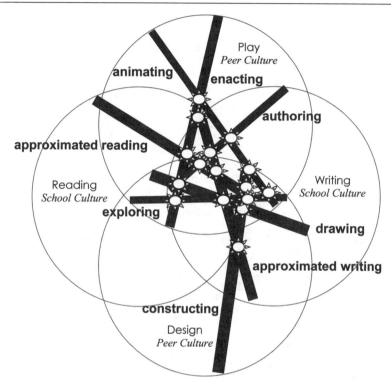

to complete teacher-modeled craft projects). Although this diagram represents a hypothetical classroom, an established body of research confirms debilitating effects and constricted pathways into literacy within procedurally rigid classrooms (Bloome, Puro, & Theodorou, 1989; Cazden, 1988; Larson, 2002; Martens, 1996; Mehan, 1979; Street & Street, 1991) where play and learner exploration is restricted (McIntyre, 1995; Ohanian, 2002; Olfman, 2003). The question to ask is: Who benefits when play is eliminated?

Allowing play in schools is a political move: It invites in popular culture, familial cultures, individual creativity, and social improvisation that threaten the authority of a standardized curriculum just as recognition of multiple literacies diminishes the hegemony of a single mainstream literacy. Play provides a mechanism that enables children and teachers to import and value students' familiar cultural resources as valid literacy curricula.

Figure 5.2. Nexus in a Play- and Design-Restricted Kindergarten

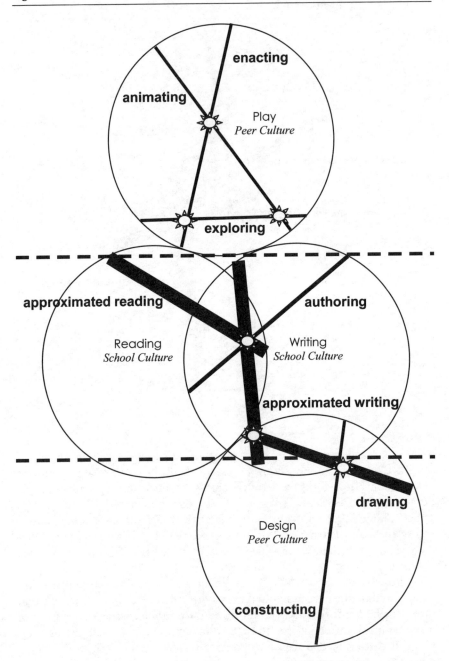

This changes how literacy functions in classrooms: from scripted standardized procedures that act as stabilizing strategies that uphold school stratifications to destabilizing tactics that allow more students to appropriate the resources they need to succeed, upsetting traditional norms and rankings of students.

Of course, political actions are not innocent. Play opens opportunities for children to resist but also to reproduce dominant patterns and discourse models, a constant tension that Abbie and the children negotiated. Play groups within peer culture tended to be stratified according to gender, race, and ethnicity. Just Guys exemplified this stratification and although the Princess Players were a more ethnically diverse group, all three groups remained fairly closed despite Abbie's active mediation, a wealth of cross-cultural experiences with families, and multicultural curricular themes and children's literature. Once constructed, the social histories within the class were durable and much slower to change than the children's dynamic use of materials.

Play offers release from social and material constraints by imagining new realities beyond typical practices. With teacher mediation, Lin did finally play her way into the Just Guys group by the end of the school year. After the boys finally recognized Lin's advanced skill with paper airplanes, Adam and then Marshall regularly asked her to join their table and to teach them new airplane folds, origami, and Chinese characters. For Princess Players, design provided a way to make play improvisations more lasting by transforming temporary play performances into concrete identity texts that marked cultural capital and reshaped classroom play groups.

PLAY AS A LITERACY AND A TACTIC

The meaning and identity transformations in this kindergarten suggest several paths for revaluing play as a literacy and a tactic.

- Bring back play as a key curricular element in early childhood classrooms as a first step. This step depends upon seeing children's personal histories and cultural knowledge as important resources for literacy. Further, creativity and critique need time to develop. Critical revision of children's play texts and designs occurred over days as children replayed texts and rewrote their favorite themes. This suggests that learners need sustained and regular blocks of time for play, so that players can return to projects to develop more complex storylines for play themes and continue the improvisation/revision process.
- Provide space for play with popular media toys and technologies. In the current play-unfriendly climate, popular culture is especially

suspect. Marsh's (2006) work with pre-service teachers showed that they resisted integrating popular culture media into school curricula, believing media themes and toys to be inappropriate for school. But by banning popular culture and toys from our classrooms, we take ourselves out of the conversation, ceding our influence to corporations and missing opportunities for critique and engaged learning.

> As teachers, we have allowed ourselves to be burdened with an increasingly earnest and accountable top-down curriculum, set in stone, while we have let Murdoch and Disney, like Pied Pipers, steal the hearts of children and monopolize pleasure. We have banished play from school and are selling the children to toy multinationals who are leading a merry trail of buy, buy, buy. There must be an alternative. . . . In disappearing from school, playfulness took with it the opportunities for personal projection and identification, the negotiating space where anything could be made to happen, which used to make curriculum friendly and resonant. (Pompe, 1996, pp. 118–119)

- Incorporate play as a catalyst for critique in critical literacy or media literacy curricula. A limitation in literature-based critical literacy activities is a tendency to elicit rational critique in class discussions that stops at the classroom door and has no enduring impact on children's patterns of social interaction. Play, on the other hand, allows children to walk around in restrictive cultural practices and identity texts and these enactments can prompt critique, improvisation, and revision of embodied practices. However, play does not automatically produce critique. In a media-intensive textual environment, children need opportunities to become critical readers and players of commercial messages ranging from a text message to a video game to animated films. Children can also participate in developing critical media literacy curricula around their media interests that are culturally responsive as well as creative and productive.
- Critically engage children's toys and media through research and teacher study groups. The recognition of the value of popular media toys as literacy resources and significant means for social positioning raises concerns about our willingness and ability to mediate popular-culture texts with gendered messages. As early literacy teachers, researchers, and teacher-educators, we need to educate ourselves about popular culture and self-critically examine our own assumptions about media and gender so that we can help children critically read toys as texts.

- Develop research designs and methods to meet the challenge of tracking children's social practices and dynamic meanings of toys and artifacts. Research methods and models need to expand to enable analysis of the materiality of multimodal texts and socially situated activity in the surrounding context. For example, critical sociocultural activity models capture multiple aspects of literacy practices and allow examination of social actors, practices, and discourses (Lewis, Enciso, & Moje, 2007). The research design used here added a material dimension and a social semiotic lens to examine the design elements of toys and child-made artifacts situated in power relations. Embodied literacies and layered identity texts with sedimented identities require an expansion of theoretical models and research designs that can simultaneously consider multiple layers in multimodal texts and map discourses, identities, practices, and meanings across a sequence of time-spaces that weave in and out of pretend and real-world contexts.

- Finally, and most important, redefine play as a literacy, a key component of "new basics" (Dyson, 2006) in early childhood education and in 21st-century literacies. This redefinition itself is a tactic for empowering teachers to reclaim curricular space in their classrooms. Policymakers who recognize that governments and industries need people who are adept at flexible creativity and innovation will value the practices that play uniquely provides: improvising with new technologies and practices, inventing new uses for materials, and imagining new contexts, spaces, and possibilities.

Methodology—Researching Literacies in a Playful Kindergarten

On one level, the classroom portrait in this book shows how a play-based approach to literacy fuses new literacy values with existing educational structures that are familiar to many early childhood teachers (e.g., play centers, writing workshop). This research depended upon a teacher-researcher partnership, and all the complexities it entails. Abbie and I met regularly throughout the year to debrief following the morning session, often over pint-sized cartons of milk and school lunches. More often than not in our discussions, we found ourselves nodding in complete agreement over the events of the morning. Abbie and I share many similarities. Like me, Abbie is a middle-aged, middle-class woman of European-American Midwestern descent. At the time, she had 17 years' teaching experience in preschool and kindergarten classrooms with a master's degree in developmental reading; I had 20 years of early childhood classroom teaching experience, and was working toward a doctoral degree in language, literacy, and culture. But these bare statistics minimally convey our relative positions. We met 2 years before this study, as Abbie was finishing her degree in an inquiry-based curriculum course where I was interning as a teaching assistant. In that class, I was impressed by her strong constructivist beliefs and the seamless integration of play and literacy that permeated her reflective journal. During the 18 months that I spent in her classroom after the study began, our connection as colleagues and friends grew as we shared classroom stories, pored over the artwork in her rich collection of children's literature, chuckled at kindergarten jokes, and fumed over frustrating educational policies. However, this collegiality carries potential hazards for research. In order to guard against possible blind spots, I needed to self-consciously and regularly examine our teacher/researcher relationship, including my beliefs about Abbie as a teacher, about myself as a teacher and researcher, and about kindergarten teaching in general. I also depended upon Abbie to fill in the blanks as we caught up on classroom events between my visits. To check my interpretations and to clarify puzzling developments, Abbie periodically read and responded to my raw field notes and video summaries, penciling her comments and insights in the margins. In turn, I tried to give back and be helpful when possible, by pitching in as an extra adult on projects or by providing technical support for children's filmmaking projects but mostly by staying out of the way of the playing and learning in this bustling kindergarten.

At another level, the book introduces and demonstrates several analytic approaches for researching literacy practices and classroom power relations as discursive activity. Discursive analysis of children's play requires innovative analytical tools and research methods capable of capturing the fluid nature of imaginary identities and pretended contexts. The action-oriented methods presented in this book offer fresh ways of looking at classroom activity, discourses, and artifacts that uncover the embodied and visual meanings produced when children play as they read and write. These methods also support critical analyses of the tactics that children use as they wield toys, books, and other objects to imagine identities and maintain their play spaces.

This syncretic approach to discourse analysis combines three critical approaches that are also embodied and action-oriented: mediated discourse analysis (Scollon, 2001a; Scollon & Scollon, 2004), multimodal analysis (Jewitt, 2006; Kress, 2003a, 2009; Norris, 2004, 2006), and critical discourse analysis (Gee, 1999). An activity model design (Figure A.1) links the three methods of analysis in this research: mediated discourse analysis of actions and practices (MDA), multimodal discourse analysis of modes (MMA), and critical discourse analysis (CDA) of discourses and identities. This three-pronged analytic approach depends upon detailed ethnographic description of children's interactions with objects in the physical environment and a video record of their interaction and social participation with peers and teachers within the learning community.

Figure A.1. Literacies and Discourse Methods in an Activity Model Research Design

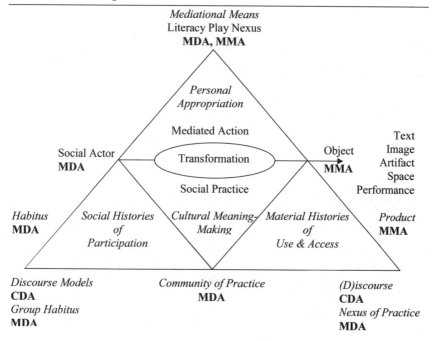

Mediated Discourse Analysis and the Playing/Reading Nexus

MEDIATED DISCOURSE ANALYSIS (MDA)

Mediated discourse analysis closely observes participants' activity, seeking their perspectives on the issues they find most critical.[1] A funnel design sifts through ethnographic data to identify the social practices significant to the issues that are central within the community (Scollon, 2001a), in this case the issues around literacy play in an era of accountability (Wohlwend, 2009a). The first filter seeks the best locations for studying how knowledgeable participants use mediating tools to engage the issue or concern; this filter located Abbie's classroom as a rich site for studying literacy play. Next, careful observation of key scenes discovers the specific practices and materials that are most often used to produce meanings. In Abbie's classroom, children typically read big books and charts in Family Circle, drew and constructed art projects at the art table, and wrote at the writing table; they played in all these places as well as in the housekeeping corner and the dollhouse. The focus in the third filter narrows to examine specific instances when key practices intersect and form nexuses that signal insider status; the nexus of reading and playing practices promoted ideals for doing school. Nexuses are further screened in the fourth filter to locate transformative events that alter meanings and identities; in this case, transformations that affected children's participation in the classroom community. Finally, fine-grained microethnographic analysis (Bloome, Carter, Christian, Otto, & Shuart-Faris, 2004) of these transformative events revealed shifts of identities and meanings by tracking children's verbal interaction, nonverbal actions, and aspects of the surrounding context such as shared classroom histories, arrangement of the physical environment, and actors' body movements, handling of materials, and gaze. (For a detailed description of the ethnographic filters and procedures in the mediated discourse analysis of literacy play activity in Abbie's classroom, see Wohlwend, 2009b.)

In order to trace how children's play and reading practices worked with and against the authority of the text to transform meanings and positionings, mediated discourse analysis of turn-by-turn mediated actions was needed to identity how play roles signaled classroom identities and reading practices that indexed teacher nurture and child need. (See Table B.1 for a transcript that documents action and talk in 25 consecutive turns during a 2-minute segment excerpted from the 11-minute Three Little Pigs storytelling event. Numbered actions cited in the analysis of this event refer to corresponding action turns in the transcript.) To examine how reading practices and story interpretations interacted with children's play goals, I looked closely at three moments when Adam's mediated action *framing a word* contrasted with Lubna's mediated action *gazing at an image* to see how Lubna's inventive reading and play-based mediation supported Adam's close approximations of print.

The first moment (actions 1–15) revealed the contrast in the two children's approaches to reading as they tackled the problem of "getting stuck" and attempted contradictory mediated actions. Adam mediated print on the page by isolating a word for closer visual inspection, focusing on the grapho-phonic details of the text. He framed the word *Once,* first making an "O" with his mouth (action 3), which didn't help him decode its initial /w/ sound, and then pinning it down for closer inspection by placing a finger on the O (action 5). He didn't apply his knowledge of the story's events or draw upon his repertoire of remembered openings for folktales that might lead him into "Once upon a time . . .". In contrast, Lubna focused on the holistic meaning of the text. She mediated the illustration on the page by inventing a phrase to narrate the image and mediated the print for Adam by recommending verbal improvisation (action 6). She leaned over the top of the book, looked briefly at the upside-down print, and advised Adam to look (at the picture) and "just say something," to just "make it up" (action 7). Adam tried out Lubna's advice and, with her support, used the strategy of inventing text. He invented a phrase, "The mom pig said," but then stalled. Lubna quickly invented a few lines for him (actions 11–14) and, bolstered by her help, Adam used his own approximations of the text to read through the first two pages of the book.

In the second instance (actions 16–20), Adam closely scrutinized the word and rejected Lubna's help in order to preserve the authority of the printed word. In action 16, Adam stopped to look closely at a second troublesome word, *found.* Lubna tried her prompting strategies again and began to read with him to get him started (action 17). However, her suggestion of "He" does not match the visual information on the page: Adam knows the configuration of letters on the page does not spell *He* and he asserts his independence as a reader and pulls the book away from the pretend teacher.

The third time Adam stopped (actions 21–25), he shifted his attention from print to image and noticed a discrepancy between the book's illustration and the flannelboard retelling. He saw that the first little pig pictured on page 2 of the book did not match the flannelboard pig (Abbie had traced the book's illustrations to make the characters) that Amy placed on the straw house. At first, Adam had difficulty drawing Lubna's attention to the mismatch; she believed that he was having trouble identifying the word *hay*. Finally, Adam was able to point out the differences in the pigs' clothing and Lubna agreed to make a switch, removing the misplaced third pig character from the flannelboard. In this reversal of roles, Adam acted as the mediator and positioned Lubna as the apprentice; Adam mediated the text for Lubna by helping her focus on details in the illustrations that anchored the story's meaning.

This episode represents one of countless peer mediation experiences that typified playing and reading in Family Circle. In this mediation-centric classroom where children were encouraged to play as they read, such play- and peer-scaffolded learning was common—and instructionally valuable. During Writers' Workshop and Choice Time, children consulted and assisted each other before seeking out Abbie or other adults—unless an adult was already immediately available. In the Abbie Wannabes group, peer mediation was further legitimated by play identities as play teachers taught their students. In this way, Lubna's strong grasp of the story meaning and her role in the school play scenario allowed her to mediate and support Adam's reading of the text.

Table B.1. Transcript of Excerpt from Three Little Pigs Literacy Play

	Action/Context	Talk	Classroom Identity	Play Identity	Effect on Meaning	Effect on Participation
1	Lubna cues Adam, pronouncing words slowly as if reading the title.	Lubna: "Three Little Pigs."*		Lubna as Teacher introducing the story	Restates title, establishes authority of original text, restarts book-reading frame	Start play: Lubna as leader of the group in control of text and start/stop of play
2	Lubna cues Adam, who is holding the book open to the first page, then points at him. Printed text on page 1: Once upon a time, there were three little pigs. They lived with their mother. One day, the mother pig said, Little Pigs, you are big now. You must build your own houses.	Lubna: [Sing-song] "And the mama says . . ." [normal voice] You're supposed to read it!	Lubna as mediator/ teacher Adam as apprentice reader	Lubna as Teacher prompts Adam as student	Improvised opening based on illustration and the array of characters placed on the flannelboard	Implicit and explicit directive by Lubna as leader and Adam as follower

* Quotation marks enclose words that represent a child's reading of the print and pictures in the book

3	Adam looks at the page, opens his mouth, closes his mouth, flips the first page around to show Lubna and back to himself as she cues him again.	Lubna: [rising intonation to invite completion] "And the mama says . . ."	Lubna as mediator Adam as apprentice reader	Lubna as Teacher prompting Adam as student	Repeats improvised opening; omits opening sentence, first paragraph	Implicit directive [for sentence completion] by Lubna as leader; Adam as expected follower
4	Lubna straightens the three pig characters, which form a line to the left of the mother pig.	Lubna: I'll help you read it.	Lubna as competent reader; Adam as "stuck" reader	Lubna as nurturing teacher Adam as needy		Peer mediation offer by Lubna as cooperative friend
5	Adam brings the book closer and rests it on his knee, and puts his finger on the word "Once," the first word in the top line of the book.	Adam: Okay. I don't know that word.	Adam as apprentice reader	Lubna as nurturing teacher/ Adam as needy child	Attempts to decode print: "Once" Restores authority of printed text	Acceptance of need for help; take-up of Lubna's offer of mediation

	Action	Speech	Role (as player)	Role (in/out of character)	Function	Analysis
6	Lubna crawls forward across the flannelboard, on all fours, to look over the top of the book at the page, which is upside-down from her point of view. Lubna smiles encouragingly at Adam. Adam lowers the book and smiles.	Lubna: When I don't know a word, I just, I just say something, I just say it!	Lubna as inventive reader and mediator; Lubna as cooperative friend	Out of character, as self	Authority of text meaning: attend to flow of story; advises invention	Peer mediation: personal experience example; advice by Lubna as cooperative friend
7	Lubna smiles encouragingly at Adam. Adam lowers the book and smiles.	Lubna: Don't look and make it up.	Lubna as inventive reader; Lubna as cooperative friend	Out of character, as self	Permission to alter text: Promotes authoring own version of text	Directive by Lubna
8	Amy leans forward, touches the first pig character, and talks to Lubna.	Amy: [babyish] You—I—I'm the three little pigs, you guys.	Amy as player	Amy as Third Little Pig	Return to storytelling and play frame	Amy makes bid to resume play; appeal for inclusion in Lubna and Adam subgroup

#	Nonverbal action	Transcript				
9	Lubna grins and rocks forward in a wolf-like lunge and Amy rolls onto her back, wiggling her feet into the air.		Lubna as player	Lubna as Big Bad Wolf	Lubna as wolf resumes play	Take-up of Amy's appeal for inclusion; initiates play with Amy
10	Adam holds the book up in front of his face and begins to read softly.	Adam: The mom pig said—	Adam as inventive reader		Reading with meaning focus; paraphrasing; skips/omits first paragraph	Joins play with Lubna and Amy
11	Lubna sits back on her heels and glances at Colin who is lying on his stomach with hands supporting his chin. She looks back at Adam.	Lubna: "The mama pig (xxx)"—I'll read it with you, okay, Adam?	Lubna as mediator/reader corrects Adam as apprentice reader	Lubna as nurturing teacher/ Adam as needy student	Establishes Lubna's invented version as the correct form; paraphrasing	Lubna as leader checks that Colin is still following. Lubna as leader and cooperative peer, Adam as follower
12		Adam: Okay.	Adam as apprentice reader	Lubna as teacher/ Adam as student		Lubna as leader, Adam as follower

13	Adam looks back at the book and Lubna removes the mother pig.	"I'm thinkin' about a old, old house." Now you read, Adam.	Lubna as mediator/inventive reader Adam as apprentice reader	Lubna as teacher/Adam as student	Innovation on text: Added new theme of old, old house	Adam and Lubna as readers playing school; Amy and Colin's movement establishes a subgroup playing the Three Little Pigs away from the flannelboard
14	Adam turns to the next page. Lubna crawls forward across the flannelboard to look at the new pages. Amy crawls behind Lubna to rummage through the pile of felt pieces and picks up the gray house. Colin joins her.	Adam: Okay.	Adam as apprentice reader		Take-up of Lubna's removal of mother pig as cue to move story forward. Turning of page accepts "I'm thinkin' about a old, old house" as substitution for text on first page	
15	Colin reaches for the red felt house and announces in a sing-song character voice.	I live in a brick house.	Colin as active player	Colin as Third Little Pig	Emphasis on meaning of text: Paraphrased dialogue	Subgroup play

16	Lubna turns back to the flannelboard and removes the second and third pigs. Adam begins again reading softly but stops to look more closely at the word *found*.	Adam: "The first pig builded his house— The first pig—"	Adam as approximating reader	Lubna as teacher; Adam as narrator	[Book Text: The first pig found some straw so he built his house of straw.] Emphasis on print	Lubna as leader
17	Lubna repeats his phrase, inserting the word *little*.	"The first little pig . . ." Do you know the rest?	Lubna as inventive reader	Lubna as nurturing teacher/ Adam as needy child	Emphasis on the meaning, not the print	Lubna as leader, Adam as follower
18	Adam touches the word *found* on the second page.	Adam: I don't know this word.	Adam as approximating reader	Adam as narrator	Emphasis on the print; meaning interrupted	Lubna as leader, Adam as follower
19	Holding the crumpled pigs in her hand, Lubna comes around beside Adam to look at the page again.	You can do it. [As if reading] "He (xx)—"	Lubna as reader/ mediator prompting Adam as apprentice	Lubna as nurturing teacher/ Adam as needy child	Emphasis on the meaning, not the print	Lubna as leader, Adam as follower
20	Adam flops his arms to his sides, sweeping the book to the floor, away from Lubna.	Adam: No!	Adam as independent reader	Adam as self	Emphasis on the print, meaning and play interrupted	Play stopped by Adam; resists Lubna as leader

21	Amy puts the yellow straw house on the flannelboard. Adam glances at the straw house in the book and over at the pig, noticing that the pig on the flannelboard is the wrong pig according to the illustration on page 2.	Adam: No, no. The first one is . . .	Adam as independent reader	Amy as First Little Pig	Emphasis on illustrations and visual detail	Amy continues play Adam as independent agent; Lubna as leader
22	Lubna points to the picture of straw and Adam objects.	Lubna: Hay! Adam: No!	Lubna as inventive reader; Adam as independent reader	Lubna as teacher, prompting	Emphasis on illustrations and visual detail	Lubna as leader; Adam as independent agent
23	Adam puts his forearm up to block Lubna as he rechecks the picture in the book. He reaches for one of the pigs that Lubna is holding. They both tug at the first little pig felt character.	Lubna: No! That's our . . .	Lubna as mediator/ reader	Lubna as teacher, directing	Emphasis on illustrations and visual detail	Lubna as leader; Adam as independent agent

24	Adam points to the illustration in the book.	Adam: This one. See?	Adam as mediator/reader	Emphasis on illustrations and visual detail	Adam as leader
25	Lubna releases the pig and Adam hands it back to her. Lubna removes the errant pig from the flannelboard and sets it on the floor beside her. In her hand, she holds the pig that matches the first little pig illustration.	Lubna: Oh yeah.	Lubna as apprentice reader	Emphasis on illustrations and visual detail	Adam as leader; Lubna as follower; Adam and Lubna as cooperative friends

Multimodal Discourse Analysis and the Playing/Designing Nexus

MULTIMODAL ANALYSIS (MMA)

I use an action-based approach to multimodal analysis (Norris, 2004; Scollon & Scollon, 2003, 2004) to understand how interaction *among* modes in the playing/designing nexus produced social and spatial relationships. An expanded form of multimodal analysis maps the relationships among actions, modes, meanings, and discourses to track transformations in meanings and participation. This approach teases out modal relationships to uncover the semiotic and social effects of the tensions created by foregrounding some modes and backgrounding others (Norris, 2004; Scollon, 2001b; Scollon & Scollon, 2003, 2004) by mapping multiple modes that interact within a single event (Norris, 2004). This expanded approach includes auditory modes (e.g., spoken language, music) and visual modes (e.g., gaze, print, image) but enables more attention to action modes (e.g., posture, facial expression, object handling, gesture, touch) as well as material modes in the built environment (proxemics [near/far relationships], layout of materials and furniture).

Each mode is a lens with a different perspective on sign-making activity, providing a more complex picture as well as comparison among modes. For example, analyzing through the perspective of the gaze mode reveals the ways that students look at materials and at each other as well as the way that they are surveilled by the teacher and by the researcher. Gaze includes my own perspective, which determined the camera angles and the research gaze: Where I aimed my camera created a frame of activity with a particular point of view. Gaze turned upon people produces subjectivities and the research gaze turns subjects into objects of inquiry. The analytic power of the gaze mode reveals how foregrounding enforces a set of power relations: The subject's gaze is foregrounded as a window into what she knows, but it is the backgrounded gaze of the researcher that produces a knowable subject.

Play and design practices allow children to shift meanings, project identities, and create new signs by using multiple modes to transform an idea, object, or action across dimensions of time and space. Just Guys created new signs by:

- enacting and animating *identities* by transforming self or objects into an imagined character through embodied actions
- recontextualizing *spaces* by transforming contexts into imagined events and environments
- drawing *images* by transforming ideas or streams of auditory information into two-dimensional visual displays
- constructing *artifacts* by transforming materials into three-dimensional tactile objects

Power relations and social effects are visible at the level of modes. Close analysis of interaction among modes uncovers the ways that social interactions are affected by multimodal resonances and tensions. Norris (2004) uses the concepts of multimodal density to explain relationships among modes and to examine their interrelated effects, that is, backgrounded modes produce resonances and tensions with foregrounded modes in ways that complicate even seemingly simple interactions. *Modal density* is produced through either intensity or complexity. A mode has *modal intensity* when it is highly foregrounded in an event (e.g., the mode of speech when talking on the telephone). *Modal complexity* occurs when a mode is intricately intertwined with other modes (e.g., the mode of speech when talking accompanied by multiple action and visual modes while simultaneously preparing dinner). By determining which modes have the most density, it is possible to show which actions and practices are most socially relevant within an event, in the Just Guys' case, which actions contribute to the construction of artifacts and the maintenance of cohesive and exclusionary social space.

Mapping Modes in Paper Airplane Folding

The boys' paper airplane folding was packed with overlapping modes; Figure C.1 shows a mapping of modes within the airplane folding event. The number of different kinds of modes indicates the complexity of the event and the size of an individual circle represents the level of attention to that mode. The large size and central placement of the mode of mediated action (object handling) indicates its foregrounding during the airplane folding event; in other words, the children's attention was highly focused on the creasing of paper. The large number of circles surrounding the object handling mode indicates that this was a modally dense event made further complex by the boys' desire to collaborate, that is, children coordinated multiple modes while collaborating and making artifacts in this playing/designing nexus by sharing their gaze, talking, navigating the layout of built environment, changing proximity, moving through space, and finally coordinating mediated actions. Each mode is considered separately followed by a closer look to see how multiple modes interacted to uphold boys' social identities and exclusionary space.

Figure C.1. Mapping Modes in a Paper Airplane Folding Activity

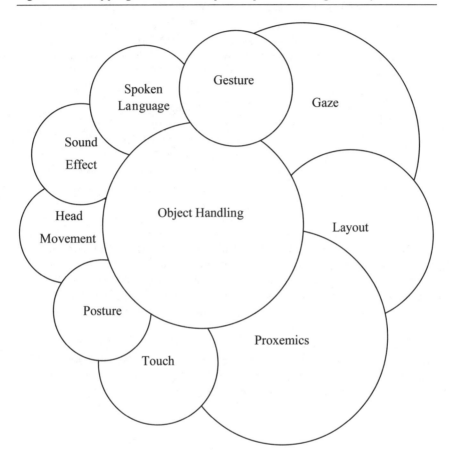

Image/Artifact

The paper airplanes can be read as layered artifacts with complex texts, with iconic, indexical, and symbolic meanings conveyed through the boys' design choices about color, shape, texture, and print:

- The jagged orange coloring on a Matt's paper airplane is iconic of flames in jet propulsion, making the folded paper more closely resemble a speeding jet.
- The white paper and folded triangular shape that forms a paper airplane indexes classroom misbehavior, signaling a familiar

cultural model in popular media: the frazzled substitute teacher who stands in front of a chaotic class, ducking chalkboard erasers and paper aircraft. Adam's worry, "But Mrs. Howard won't let us," indicates his awareness that paper airplanes don't "belong" in school (even though Abbie had never prohibited paper airplane making.)

- The shape and color of the printed letters in the word *airplane* have no iconic or indexical link to an actual aircraft but the word has been arbitrarily assigned and is conventionally accepted as its appropriate symbol (Peirce in Hartshorne, Weiss, & Burks, 1998). Marshall printed an approximation of the print symbol when he wrote "ALANE" in his title "HAW tWO MAC A PAPR ALANE" on the cover of his book.

Gaze

As Marshall taught Matt, their shared gaze on the paper airplane created an inclusive space. Proper production of the plane required Matt to carefully watch Marshall's hands for sustained periods of time. When Lin approached, each boy concentrated his gaze on his own paper and their simultaneous downward gazes jointly constructed an exclusionary space that shut her out.

The boys also gazed at one another's projects in order to evaluate and compare quality. Marshall looked critically at Matt's plane to judge the accuracy of his folds; Adam looked at Matt's and Marshall's design and noted that their airplane "just slip-slops around." Children sought each other's evaluative gaze as they proffered artifacts for inspection. Matt frequently held out his folded paper for Marshall to evaluate and correct; Marshall and Lin showed their completed planes to Abbie and a teacher associate for adult evaluation and praise; and Marshall pretended to fly his plane from one child to another to show off his creation around the classroom.

Talk

Matt's questions and requests for help positioned him as a novice while Adam used evaluative statements and directives to establish his independent competence (ability to make "the best paper airplane ever"). Adam's critiques expressed doubt about the quality of Marshall's airplane: "Does it fly good?" Most striking was the almost total absence of talk between Lin and the three boys. She walked past their table and paused to watch in silence; she briefly glanced at Marshall's plane without comment.

Layout, Proxemics, and Movement

Modal relationships between children, materials, and physical space influenced the interaction. The three boys' close physical proximity signaled their co-membership as a peer group in contrast to Lin, who worked on the same project but at a distance in a rocker turned away from them. Although the boys were in almost constant movement, they maintained close proximity with each other. They moved around the table, rarely sitting, and around the room, getting paper, pretending to fly their planes. The table anchored the boys' activity, acting as a kind of home base in their wanderings around the room. The table's location next to the paper shelf allowed easy access to the 15 or more sheets of paper the children needed as they made and discarded their numerous attempts.

Mediated Action

Marshall's speed in creating paper airplanes demonstrated his skill and made it possible for him to produce five airplanes in the time the other children each needed to create one. He quickly (4 seconds) coordinated nine actions (lengthwise fold, crease, flip, realign edges, diagonal fold, crease, flip, diagonal fold, crease) to position the paper on the table and to create the proper sequence of folds. His facility established him as group leader and allowed him to mediate for Matt and to create an airplane for Adam. The mode of mediated action was most foregrounded in this activity as airplane production required the boys to attend closely to each (and each other's) mediated action to accomplish folding.

In order to map multimodality (interaction among modes) in Just Guys' play and design practices, I combined close analysis from mediated discourse analysis with modes and modal density found through multimodal discourse analysis. (See Table C.1 for a transcript that documents action and talk in 35 consecutive turns of mediated actions during a 3-minute segment excerpted from the 21-minute paper airplane episode. Numbered actions cited in the analysis of this event refer to corresponding action turns in the transcript.)

In actions 1 through 6, Marshall and Matt's collaboration and concentration on a shared project demonstrated through their joint gaze, simultaneous handling of a common object, and dyadic question/response interactions closed off their activity to (female) newcomers such as Lin and protected their shared design activity as a classroom space for boys' topics and activities. Protection of masculine space was typical of Just Guys activity: Although Lin or other girls sometimes sat at the same table with this group and the boys might share materials and talk with them, Just Guys rarely engaged in joint projects or skill mentoring with girls. Although Adam received minimal response to his overture "What're you makin'?" in action 4, he easily joined their activity, perhaps due to tacit recognition of his prior standing as a Just Guys member. Adam displayed knowledge of the group's design standards, in an immediate declaration in which he positions himself as a skilled airplane maker, "Remember, Marshall, I'm making the best airplane ever" (action 12).

Matt's requests and Marshall's responses combined to amplify mediation across modes so that gaze, gesture, talk, and action combined produced a mediation space, a zone of proximal development, the space between what a novice can learn alone and what can be learned with the assistance of a more experienced mentor (Vygotsky, 1935/1978). Matt's requests (actions 3, 10, 13, 15, 21, 24) prompted immediate multimodal explanations, reminders, and demonstrations by Marshall that combined mediated actions, with gaze, talk, movement, and gesture (actions 3, 10, 11, 14, 16, 22, 25). Matt's actions and questions inscribed his own status as a novice paper airplane maker and Marshall's status as a design expert within the Just Guys affinity group. However, Matt made the mediation interactive by interrupting demonstrations as soon as Marshall began the fold, indicating his desire to produce the airplane himself (actions 3, 25, 35). His actions indicated a tension between independence and dependence apparent throughout the excerpt. As the sequence progressed, Marshall decreased modal density to offer less support and to transfer responsibility to Matt, verbally reminding him to remember prior moves ("Like I showed you, okay?" in action 14) and nonverbally reducing his demonstrations to allow Matt to take over: touching the place for the next fold (actions 16, 22), beginning a fold and releasing it (action 21), and even ignoring Matt's request prompting, Matt to make a solo attempt.

This analysis of mediated actions excerpted from the airplane folding session show that the resonances across modes in peer mediation and design practices produced a cohesive masculine space for displaying skills, evaluating artifacts, and competing. In this episode, Matt built a single paper airplane as Marshall mediated Matt's design process and Adam compared his airplane to theirs. The boys' shared interest in supporting and evaluating each other's mediated actions with paper strengthened their group cohesion in ways that reinforced Marshall's identity as master designer and ignored Lin and her folding expertise.

Table C.1. Transcript of Excerpt from Paper Airplanes: Actions 1–35

	Mediated Actions	Talk	Modal Density	Design Identity	Effect on Artifact	Effect on Participation
1	Marshall takes Matt's paper and nonverbally demonstrates the beginning of a fold by bringing a corner to the center fold, but then releases it so that Matt must make the fold himself. Matt suddenly sees the symmetrical pattern that repeats each fold on the opposite side of the plane. Lin walks up to the table but neither boy makes eye contact nor acknowledges her. She watches them for a few moments, gets a blank sheet of paper from the shelf, and leaves to make paper airplanes by herself.	Matt: Oh, then this one.	Folding and copied action as teaching; shared Gaze and Proximity as group cohesion; constructs exclusion-ary peer space with Zone of Proximal Development (ZPD); layout gives boys but not Lin easy access to materials	Marshall as designer, Marshall as mediator, Matt as apprentice, boys as insiders girl as outsider	Matt's copied design as concretized participation, Lin's distant copied design as detached participation or participation substitute	Lin's physical proximity as implicit bid to join play; boys' lack of eye contact or talk with her as implicit rejection boys' joint focus on same object as bond
2	Matt picks it up and creases the fold that Marshall indicated.	Marshall: And then you need to turn it. I really know how to make lots of airplanes. I have lots of airplanes.	Folding, Talk, Proximity constructs mediating relationship, ZPD Talk: Claim of skill expertise	Marshall as designer, Marshall as mediator, Matt as novice Boys as collaborators	Matt's paper as unfinished project; Marshall's airplane making skill as cultural capital	Inscribes mentoring power relations (with Marshall as leader and as design authority, Matt as follower and design novice, as passive learner who is led)

	Mediated Actions	Talk	Modal Density	Design Identity	Effect on Artifact	Effect on Participation
3	Marshall takes the airplane from Matt and bends one wing to demonstrate the next step. Matt reaches his hands in between Marshall's hands to continue the fold and take over this step. Marshall pulls his hands back to relinquish the task.	Matt: Now what do you do? O-o-::h. Now you do that.	Folding, proximity, gaze as ZPD, Talk as appeal for help	Marshall as mediator, Matt as novice	Marshall takes possession of Matt's plane in response to appeal; Matt takes over in mid-step as part of Marshall's scaffolding	Positions Marshall as active, Matt as first passive then active, Boys' joint focus on same object as bond, shared physical activity as bond
4	Adam approaches the writing table	Adam: What're you makin'?	Folding as object of talk	Adam as cooperative peer		Explicit request for information, implicit bid to join group
5	Matt answers without looking up.	Matt: Airplane	Folding as object of talk, Talk as acknowledgment; Gaze as exclusion	Matt as designer	Paper as project in progress	Acknowledges request; no explicit request needed; Adam stays
6	Marshall looks at Matt's folded paper, sees an error in his folding, begins a sentence but abandons the attempt, leaving the table mid-sentence to get a new sheet of paper for himself from the shelf.	Marshall: Yeah, but. But Matt, you need a—	Folding; Gaze as evaluation; Movement as ZPD	Marshall as evaluator and corrector	Paper as project off track	Inscribes mentoring power relations Marshall's role as Matt's mentor secondary to his role as designer of his own project

	Mediated Actions	Talk	Modal Density	Design Identity	Effect on Artifact	Effect on Participation
7	Matt steps back from the table holding the half-folded airplane in his hands as Adam follows him. Facing Matt, Adam raises a concern about making airplanes at school, arms wide, elbows bent, palms up in a "Now what?" gesture.	Adam: But Mrs. Howard won't let us.	Folding, Gesture and Talk construct peer space, activity as resistant	Teacher as monitor Boys as good students	Project as prohibited non-school activity; Tension between good boy behavior and bad boy activity	Assumption that Adam will join activity Casts teacher as opposing boys' agenda, increases group cohesion
8	Matt shifts his weight from foot to foot and begins an explanation but gets interrupted.	Matt: She made things.	Talk, Movement construct teacher authority	Teacher as tolerant, Teacher as capable Boys as good students	Project as permitted school activity	Frames boys' activity as allowed
9	Returning with a clean sheet of paper, Marshall walks directly up to the two boys and talks over Matt.	Marshall: <u>Make one</u> because Mrs. Howard doesn't know how to, right, how I make them.	Talk, Movement, Proximity: constructs boys' expert space	Marshall as teacher-endorsed expert designer	Project as permitted school activity	Marshall as specially permitted due to folding skill that surpasses teacher's
10	Adam leaves to get paper and start a plane. Matt comments as Marshall folds the paper lengthwise. Sliding his hand backward, Marshall runs his palm down the crease.	Matt: Do you have to put it [paper] that way?	Folding, Gaze, Proximity, constructs ZPD space	Marshall as mediator, Matt as novice,	Marshall's airplane as demonstration and concretized expertise	Inscribes mentoring power relations Common focus builds pair cohesion
11	Marshall then turns down one corner on a diagonal and expertly creases this edge in the same way. As Matt watches this demonstration, he crumples his airplane and leaves the table to toss it in the trash and get a new paper to start over as Adam returns.	Matt: O:h.	Folding, Gaze, Proximity as ZPD Matt's Movement as self-evaluation, Adam's Movement as joining group	Matt as inexpert novice	Matt's paper as flawed, artifact as concretized inexpertise	Inscribes mentoring power relations Tacit acceptance of Adam as member of group

	Mediated Actions	Talk	Modal Density	Design Identity	Effect on Artifact	Effect on Participation
12	Adam folds a corner of his paper, omitting the first fold and approximating the second fold. Marshall continues, making his fourth and fifth folds. The boys are at opposite ends of the table	Adam: Don't forget, Marshall, I'm makin' the best paper airplane ever.	Folding, Gaze, Proximity, Talk constructs Adam's independence Talk as in-group competition	Adam as independent expert	Adam's paper as concretized expertise; "best" paper airplane as cultural capital and marker of social rank in Just Guys group	Creates competition among group members, display of skill as social capital to increase status within group establishes Adam as competitor, group member, active learner
13	Matt returns and bends his paper by placing the two shorter sides together. He stops, and corrects himself by folding the paper lengthwise. He holds the paper up and creases it between his thumb and forefinger, then asks Marshall about the next step.	Matt: And then what do you do, Marshall?	Folding, Talk, Proximity as ZPD Gaze as independence	Matt as apprentice with emerging skill, Marshall as expert and mediator	Matt's self-correction and revised paper as concretized learning, open to evaluation and revision	Inscribes mentoring power relations Self-monitoring and revision indicates Matt's emerging skill
14	Marshall answers as Matt folds one corner diagonally, just as Marshall demonstrated. Marshall continues working on his own plane.	Marshall: Just like I showed you, okay?	Folding, Talk, Proximity as ZPD; Gaze as independence	Matt as apprentice with emerging skill, Marshall as busy designer	Reference to previous teaching demonstration	Inscribes mentoring power relations; Marshall's response transfers responsibility for remembering steps to Matt

	Mediated Actions	Talk	Modal Density	Design Identity	Effect on Artifact	Effect on Participation
15	Matt stops, looks, and asks Marshall to check this step.	Matt: And then you do this?	Folding, Talk, Proximity as ZPD; Gaze and Talk as appeal for evaluation	Matt as apprentice with emerging skill, Marshall as expert	Matt's revised paper as concretized learning, open to evaluation and revision	Inscribes mentoring power relations; Matt's recall of next step indicates emerging skill
16	Marshall leans across the table to inspect the plane and touches one corner.	Marshall: Yeah. And then you have this down there.	Folding, Gaze, Proximity as ZPD; Gesture as minimal mediation	Marshall as evaluator, Matt as apprentice with emerging skill	Paper airplane as device for peer mediation and self-mediation through symmetrical repetitions	Inscribes mentoring power relations; shared gaze and gesture maintains group cohesion; response as minimal mediation that transfers responsibility
17	Marshall leaves to show his plane to the teacher associate. Matt flips the plane and repeats the fold on the other wing.		Movement to display work and seek praise	Marshall as independent worker and good designer	Artifact as object with cultural capital as evidence of completed school task	Marshall recognized as good student who works hard and recognizes adult authority
18	In the meantime, Adam has created his own plane using a series of diagonal folds, using a different method that produces a cross between a paper fan and an airplane.		Folding, Gaze, lack of Talk, and Proximity as independence but within group	Adam as inventive novice, Adam as independent designer	Project as invention; paper as approximation of paper airplane	Lack of request for mediation constructs Adam as independent agent; presence at table as group member but not in overt ZPD

#	Mediated Actions	Talk	Modal Density	Design Identity	Effect on Artifact	Effect on Participation
19	Adam walks his plane across the room to show Marshall. Adam points to the center crease in his plane and flicks his wrist to pretend that it is flipping upside down.	Adam: Inside out Lookit. See, I'm makin' the best paper airplane ever.	Movement, Gaze, Gesture, Talk as display of skill, competition	Marshall as designer, Adam as designer	Completed artifacts as concretized skills and creativity that enable comparison and evaluation of quality of planes as toys	Adam demonstration with assertion along with his evaluation positions Adam and Marshall as equal group members
20	Adam looks at Marshall's plane and both boys return to the table.		Movement, Gaze, Layout			Evaluation of Marshall's plane, possibly as template
21	Matt again asks for help. Marshall demonstrates one more fold: He begins and releases the final fold on one of the wings. Matt makes this fold but does not make a matching crease on the other wing, resulting in a lopsided plane.	Matt: Then what do you do, Marshall? I forgot.	Folding, Gaze, Talk as ZPD	Matt as confused novice, Marshall as mediator	Project as stalled; problem in need of expert	Inscribes mentoring power relations and maintains pair cohesion; novice as lost without mentor's step-by-step guidance, proximity, and gaze
22	Matt walks the plane to Marshall on his way to get more paper, who briefly looks at it and touches the wing that needs to be creased.		Movement and Proximity: following as request for help; Gaze and gesture as mediation, ZPD	Matt as apprentice with emerging skill, Marshall as expert mediator	Paper airplane as set of previously demonstrated steps	Inscribes mentoring power relations and maintains pair cohesion; implicit directive to perform next step

	Mediated Actions	Talk	Modal Density	Design Identity	Effect on Artifact	Effect on Participation
23	Matt follows Marshall around the table, protesting. Marshall does not respond.	Matt: I forgot how to do it, though.	Movement and Proximity as following with Talk as explicit request for ZPD	Matt as novice, Marshall as mediator	Paper airplane as set of unknown steps	Matt's repetition of forgotten step and need for more overt help emphasizes his status as beginner
24	Matt places the plane on the table and begins a fold on the wrong side.	This way?	Folding as request for evaluation	Matt as apprentice with emerging skill	Paper airplane as experiment, fold as potential next step	Marshall's lack of response requires this independent attempt by Matt and rejects a novice status for Matt
25	Without a word, Marshall begins the fold and Matt takes the plane back to finish the crease on the wing.	Matt: Oh-h.	Folding as mediation; Talk and folding as following, ZPD	Matt resumes role as apprentice with emerging skill, Marshall as mediator	Paper airplane as instructional; project back on track	Acceptance of need to scaffold by Marshall; move toward independence by Matt; inscribes mentoring power relations and maintains pair cohesion
26	Marshall begins his fourth plane.	Marshall: I love makin' paper airplanes. I made hundreds.	Folding, Talk as display of skill, competition	Marshall as avid and prolific designer	Paper airplane as affinity object and cultural capital	Fourth plane concretizes design proficiency

	Mediated Actions	Talk	Modal Density	Design Identity	Effect on Artifact	Effect on Participation
27	Adam makes the first fold on another plane.	Adam: Yeah, I love to. That's my favorite thing in the whole wide world to do, on my list.	Folding, Talk as display of shared affinity	Adam as avid designer with many other interests	Paper airplane as affinity object in Just Guys group	Establishes importance of ranking activities in a list of favorites
28	Matt holds up his partially folded plane, asking Marshall to inspect it.	Matt: Is this the paper airplane?	Artifact, Talk as request for Gaze and evaluation of Folding, ZPD	Matt as apprentice, Marshall as expert evaluator	Paper airplane as possibly complete, waiting for endorsement	Inscribes mentoring power relations and maintains pair cohesion
29	Adam shakes his head.	Adam: That just slip slops around. I tried it before. At my grandma's.	Gaze, Gesture, Talk as evaluation	Adam as expert evaluator	Paper airplane as inferior design	Attempt to establish mentoring power relations between Adam and Matt
30	Matt holds the plane out to Marshall, again, for inspection.	Matt: This is the airplane?	Artifact, Talk as explicit request for Marshall's Gaze and evaluation, ZPD	Matt as apprentice with emerging skill, Marshall as the expert, not Adam	Paper airplane as possibly complete, waiting for endorsement	Rejects Adam as mentor and reinscribes mentoring power relations with Marshall
31	Marshall looks at Matt's plane, and then takes it and hands it back.	Marshall: No!	Gaze, Talk, Touch, and Artifact as evaluation	Marshall as evaluator	Airplane as error	Abruptness as directive to reject airplane and perhaps as bid to close mentoring

	Mediated Actions	Talk	Modal Density	Design Identity	Effect on Artifact	Effect on Participation
32	Matt looks at his plane.	Matt: It's not ready yet?	Gaze, Talk, and Artifact as self-evaluation	Matt as apprentice, with emerging skill	Salvages airplane from error, just not yet completed	Bid to retain airplane and restore ZPD and mentoring power relations
33	Marshall agrees, making the final crease on his own plane.	Marshall: Yeah, it's not ready yet.	Folding Gaze, Talk, and Artifact as evaluation	Matt as apprentice, with emerging skill, Marshall as designer	Airplane as almost completed	Affirmation repairs pair cohesion; agreement for need to continue ZPD and mentoring power relations
34	Marshall takes the plane and begins to make another fold.	Matt: And then what do you do?	Talk and Artifact as appeal for help	Matt as apprentice	Airplane as instructional tool	Restores mentoring power relations
35	Matt reaches in and pulls it away to make the crease himself.	Matt: That's how you make one? Oh.	Folding, Gaze and Talk as mediation, Folding and Gaze as Independence	Matt restored to apprentice with emerging skill	Airplane as completed	Inscribes mentoring power relations and Matt's emerging independence; maintains pair cohesion

Critical Discourse Analysis and the Playing/Writing Nexus

CRITICAL DISCOURSE ANALYSIS (CDA)

Critical discourse analysis (Gee, 1999) provides a theory for understanding how discourses constitute and circulate gendered identity texts, and analytic tools to link global discourses to locally situated identities in order to reveal power relations. The constitutive power of language exists in tension with pre-existing histories of objects and subjects in a place and also with potential trajectories of individuals. However, language does not wield unlimited power to create, dissolve, or transform the meanings of subjects and things. A discourse exists in tension with the "thingness of things" (Brown, 1998, p. 936), that is, a discourse shapes and is shaped by material reality, social histories, and individual action. Because of this, discourses that circulate in a classroom can be tracked through "absent others" through their sponsorship of literacy materials (Brandt & Clinton, 2002).

Consistent with the focus on practices and materials in this study, I used expanded forms of critical discourse analysis focusing on language and embodied social practices with material objects (Gee, 1999; Scollon, 2001a) to identify power relations. Play interactions are analyzed here using the analytic tool *situated identities* (Gee, 1996), subject positions that make up valid ways of being and belonging in particular discourse such as the situated identity *author* within the context of a kindergarten writing workshop. Language actively constitutes social subjects (Foucault, 1972), making particular subject positions available or unavailable to individuals; for example, discourses of consumerism and girlhood at the global level and the children's play practices at the local level constituted the situated identities Disney Princess fan and doll player just as educational discourse at the institutional level and writing workshop activity at the local level constitute the situated identities *author, director,* and *actor.* The structured analysis of identities as discrete entities should be viewed as a useful heuristic rather than a representation of actual lived lives, with the recognition that individuals enact heteroglossic (Bakhtin, 1981) identity performances that draw upon and link shared histories of social relationships and classroom power relations.

In Chapter 4, close visual analysis of Zoe's storyboard revealed several text revisions that correspond to play improvisations that are only visible through microanalysis of the video data. For example, the children's enactment of Scene 3 was confused and chaotic in live action: The dragon puffed smoke at the princess, the prince said "Get away" to the princess, and she ran away from both of them. However, microanalysis of the action in Scene 3 in Table D.1 shows Colin's challenge to Zoe's text and her struggle to maintain the integrity of her storyboard plan and her authority as director. Zoe's improvised solution preserved the meaning of her original text and maintained a more powerful role for her princess character. Scene 3 began with the dragon (Matt) breathing smoke at Princess Aurora (Zoe) and the prince (Colin) standing off to the side. Zoe fended off Colin's bid to improvise and add a character so that he could play a second fire-breathing dragon (Turn 5). Instead, she insisted that he stick to the storyboard plan and play the prince (Turn 6). In Turn 7, Colin misinterpreted Zoe's direction and threatened the dragon, saying "Get away" (with a look and body posture that implied "or else"). In Turns 8 and 9, Colin was nonplussed by Zoe's correction of his performance and her insistence that the prince warn the princess to "get away" (to flee the dragon).

The dual meanings of the text "Get away!" imply opposing contexts: In the first context, the prince shouts at and actively fights off the dragon; in the second, the prince passively stands by and shouts out a warning to the princess. The play stalled as Colin tried to puzzle out a sensible move for the prince. Encouragement by Teresa (one of the three fairies) to say "Get away!" did not clarify the meaning conflict for him. Frustrated, Zoe verbally and physically rejected Teresa's intervention as an unwarranted intrusion. This prompted a visiting pre-service teacher to step in and try to help by also directing Colin to say "Get away!" The adult intervention prevented the possibility of further talk between the children that might have allowed them to see the contradiction between the two implied contexts. Colin abandoned the attempt to make sense of the scene and advanced menacingly toward Zoe, arms raised and fingers crooked as if ready to attack. At this point, Zoe also gave up on making sense with Colin and simply ran away from him.

Further conversation between author and actor might have allowed the children to sort out text meanings and negotiate character roles. Despite the prevalence of collaborative talk about shared meanings during improvised play scenarios at the dollhouse, the players did not talk out their conflicting interpretations during this performance. Instead, Colin accepted a nonsensical script, and Zoe accepted a nonsensical performance. Perhaps Colin felt constrained by an actor's responsibility to follow the author/animator's direction and text when enacting someone else's authored play, perhaps the children recognized that this videotaping was a final performance so discussion of the scene would not be in keeping with a polished run-through, or perhaps they felt that any attempt to further discuss the scene would disobey the teacher associate's implicit direction to get on with the performance. Fortunately, Zoe quickly improvised a way to restore the meaning of her original text by replaying Scene 1 with Emma (see turns 16 and 17 in Table D.1). The replaying of the chase scene reestablishes Maleficent (Emma's character) as the primary threat to the princess and glosses over Colin's misplayed line as an attacking prince. At several points in the play, similar impromptu transformations by Zoe created a way to keep the play moving forward while maintaining the meaning of both her storyboard and the original film.

Table D.1. Transcript of Scene 3 in *Sleeping Beauty* Play: Turns 1–17

Turn	Action/Context	Talk at each turn	Transformation: Classroom identity	Transformation: Play identity	Effect on meaning; Script text	Effect on participation
1	Zoe is directing and playing the lead in the *Sleeping Beauty* play that she has written. She refers to her storyboard to locate the next scene.	Zoe: The next scene is . . .		Author, animator, and lead actor	Transition between scenes; text suspended	Zoe's role as playwright/ animator establishes her leader role. She has chosen the players; their positions as characters require them to follow her directions
2	Zoe shouts to the cast clustered around the bicycle racks.	Zoe: Okay!	Zoe as animator		Play resumes	Everyone attends to Zoe
3	She points to Matt and then turns her back to him, arms rigid at her sides. She continues to watch him by looking back over her shoulder.	Zoe: You're blowing steam on me, behind me.	Zoe as animator and actor, Matt as actor	Zoe as Princess, Matt as Dragon	Scene 3: The Dragon threatens the Princess	Zoe directs Matt
4	Matt puffs in one continuous motion at her neck and back, slightly wiggling his head back and forth.		Matt as actor	Matt as attacking Dragon; Zoe as Princess	In-character action, consistent with script	Complies with Zoe's directive
5	Colin steps next to Matt and puffs out his cheeks as if to blow steam.	Colin: Now me.	Colin as improvising author/player	Bid for new role as second Dragon	Challenges authority of text with innovation	Bids for turn to play according to own improvised script

Turn	Action/Context	Talk at each turn	Transformation: Classroom identity	Transformation: Play identity	Effect on meaning: Script text	Effect on participation
6	Zoe points at Colin.	Zoe: No, not you. You're the Prince. You say, "Get away."	Asserts Zoe's authority as animator and author	Restates play identity: Colin as Prince	Establishes authority of text by citing assigned role and line from script	Rejects bid for turn to play;. implicit directive to comply with script
7	Colin looks at Matt, lowers his head, and leans toward Matt.	Colin: "Get away."	Accepts Zoe's authority as leader	Colin as defending Prince, Matt as Dragon who is a threat	Prince commands Dragon to leave; complies with text's wording	Complies with Zoe's directive
8	Zoe laughs and points at Matt, then herself.	Zoe: No! Not to him! [To] Me!	Zoe uses her authority as author to clarify the meaning of the text.	Colin as Prince telling Princess to escape, Zoe as Princess who needs to flee	Prince warns Princess; tells her to run; clarifies the implicit meaning of the text not recorded in the words	Rejects Colin's compliant action; implicit directive to repeat action in a revised way
9	Colin straightens and stands still, looks at Zoe, puzzled.	Colin: [Implicit request for help by gaze at leader combined with inaction]	Colin as actor; Zoe as animator	Play stalls	Discrepancy between text and two contexts: Conflict in implicit meanings of words "Get away!"	No take-up of directive to repeat action

Turn	Action/Context	Talk at each turn	Transformation: Classroom identity	Transformation: Play identity	Effect on meaning; Script text	Effect on participation
10	Teresa steps in between Zoe and Colin and repeats Zoe's finger-pointing demonstration. She smiles at him and gestures for him to "go ahead" by sweeping her hands forward toward Zoe and Matt.	Teresa: [Say] "Get away!"	Teresa as cooperative friend; Zoe as leader	Colin as Prince	Reinforces explicit wording but does not address the confusion of two implicit meanings	Affirms Zoe's directive; supports Colin with encouragement
11	Zoe rushes toward Teresa and shakes her finger at her.	Zoe: You're not—	Zoe as animator, Teresa as actor usurping animator role	Teresa as Third Fairy telling Prince to get away	Unwarranted appearance of character not in scene	Rejects Teresa's support
12	Zoe looks back at Colin, as Teresa tells Colin with a sweeping gesture, palm up, outward toward Zoe.	Teresa: Say it again, "Get away."	Teresa as animator, Colin as actor	Teresa out of character	Focus on verbalization of surface text, not meaning	Reaffirms Zoe's directive; supports Colin with encouragement
13	Zoe gives Teresa a slight push and points a finger at her.	Zoe: Be quiet.	Zoe as animator; Teresa as competing animator	Teresa out of character	Play suspended	Directive with aggressive action, conflict
14	The teacher associate steps closer. Zoe looks up guiltily and opens her mouth to explain, but the teacher associate talks to Colin.	Teacher: Say "Get away."	Colin as obedient student; teacher associate as animator and adult in authority	Reinforces Zoe's authority as child animator, Colin's compliance as actor	Teacher legitimates explicit wording, fails to see/address confusion over implicit meanings; forestalls further discussion of meanings	Adult's directive prevents further conflict; enforces Colin's compliance; reinforces Zoe's role as leader; ignores Teresa's contribution.

Turn	Action/Context	Talk at each turn	Transformation: Classroom identity	Transformation: Play identity	Effect on meaning: Script text	Effect on participation
15	Colin crouches down, menacingly with clawing hand motions, reaches forward and growls the words at Zoe.	Colin: "Get away."	Colin as actor	Colin as Prince attacking Princess	Text misinterpreted / transformed: Prince threatens Princess	Colin performs compliantly; gives up sense-making
16	Zoe gives up on directing Colin and runs away from him toward the grassy playground and shouts behind her, pointing to Emma.	Zoe: Okay! Now, Emma, chase me again!	Zoe as animator, Emma as actor	Zoe as Princess, Emma as Bad Guy	Transforms text by adding new scene that replays Scene 1 with original threat; clarifies Bad Guy as threat, rather than Prince.	Zoe gives up sense-making with Colin; resumes directing and engages Emma
17	Emma chases Zoe across the grass and back to the sidewalk in a wide arc.		Zoe as actor, Emma as actor	Zoe as Princess, Emma as Bad Guy	Text transformed with meaning restored by addition of replayed scene	

Notes

Chapter 1

1. All names in the book, including the children, the teacher, the doctor, the university football team among others, are pseudonyms.

2. For information on research methods and checklists in the search for a play-rich literacy classroom and locating an appropriate site for ethnographic analysis, see Wohlwend, 2007b.

3. Benchmarks included elements from Clay's Observation Survey (1993), including letter and word recognition, concepts about print, writing vocabulary, and running records of leveled texts.

4. Literacy practices, like all social practices, do not occur in isolation nor are they neatly delineated. However, for the purposes of looking closely at overlapping literacies and demonstrating the semiotic power of play, I bracket reading, writing, play, and design practices here by the use of print, image, artifacts, and performances as well as by the use of materials and locations.

5. For coding purposes, I named the three groups according to their shared play interests.

Chapter 2

1. Lave and Wenger (1991) problematize the idea of classrooms as communities of practice, arguing that school does not operate as a true apprenticeship to cultural activity in the adult workplace; rather, the structure and activity of school teaches children to take up positions that are valued only within the field of schooling. However, I argue that a kindergarten acts as an apprenticeship into a 13+ year career as student, a significant portion of a lifetime, so it's worth understanding how classrooms operate as childhood communities of practice.

2. Following Jeffersonian transcription conventions, colons (::) are used following a letter to indicate an elongated speech sound; [xxx] represents undistinguishable words.

Chapter 3

1. For the purposes of teasing out practices and supporting mediated actions for close analysis in this study, I used the term *design* to refer to practices that produce images and artifacts and the term *writing* to refer to practices that produce printed or handwritten text. However, in lived lives, the boundaries are blurred and printed pages, images, and artifacts all constitute multimodal texts; reading a single line of print involves multiple modes. I also intend my use of the term *design* to be consistent with social semiotic definitions (Kress, 1997; New London Group, 1996) in which design refers to planful action that appropriates conventions and reconfigures power relations.

Chapter 4

1. Pocahontas Barbie, barefoot and dressed in buckskin, is the exception as the doll communicates a child-of-nature, romanticized waif identity (Giroux, 1997).

2. Filmmaking activities were not videotaped or analyzed in the study as they involved adult-directed activity and occurred outside the classroom.

3. Niko's two invented chants have four stressed syllables per line, a structure that follows meter conventions for accentual verse common in children's playground chants and nursery rhymes (http://www.danagioia.net/essays/eaccentual.htm).

Appendix B

1. The tacit and pervasive nature of social practices requires careful examination of hidden assumptions and self-reflexivity on the part of the researcher. A collaborative research stance works to make assumptions and motives transparent, hopefully in ways that flatten power relations and further participants' goals as well as those of the researchers.

References

Adler, M. (2008, September 1). Why test NYC kindergartners? *All Things Considered.* Retrieved June 7, 2009, from http://www.npr.org/templates/story/story.php?storyId=94176236

Auwarter, M. (1986). Development of communicative skills: The construction of fictional reality in children's play. In J. Cook-Gumperz, W. A. Corsaro, & J. Streeck (Eds.), *Children's worlds and children's language* (pp. 205–230). New York: Mouton de Gruyter.

Baker-Sperry, L., & Grauerholz, L. (2003). The pervasiveness and persistence of the feminine beauty ideal in children's fairy tales. *Gender & Society, 17*(5), 711–726.

Bakhtin, M. M. (1981). *The dialogic imagination: Four essays.* Austin, TX: University of Texas Press.

Bateson, G. (1955/1972). A theory of play and fantasy. In G. Bateson (Ed.), *Steps to an Ecology of Mind* (pp. 177–193). San Francisco: Chandler.

Bauman, R., & Briggs, C. L. (1990). Poetics and performance as critical perspective on language and social life. *Annual Reviews of Anthropology, 19,* 59–88.

Blackburn, M. V. (2005). Disrupting dichotomies for social change: A review of, critique of, and complement to current educational literacy scholarship on gender. *Research in the Teaching of English, 39*(4), 398–416.

Blaise, M. (2005a). A feminist poststructuralist study of children "doing" gender in an urban kindergarten classroom. *Early Childhood Research Quarterly, 20*(1), 85–108.

Blaise, M. (2005b). *Playing it straight: Uncovering gender discourses in the early childhood classroom.* New York: Routledge.

Bloome, D., Carter, S. P., Christian, B. M., Otto, S., & Shuart-Faris, N. (2004). *Discourse analysis and the study of classroom language and literacy events: A microethnographic perspective.* Mahwah, NJ: Lawrence Erlbaum.

Bloome, D., Katz, L., Solsken, J., Willett, J., & Wilson-Keenan, J.-A. (2000). Interpellations of family/community and classroom literacy practices. *Journal of Educational Research, 93*(3), 155–163.

Bloome, D., Puro, P., & Theodorou, E. (1989). Procedural display and classroom lessons. *Curriculum Inquiry, 19*(3), 265–291.

Boldt, G. M. (2001). Failing bodies: Discipline and power in elementary class-rooms. *Journal of Curriculum Theorizing, 17*(4), 91–104.

Boldt, G. M. (2002). Toward a reconceptualization of gender and power in an elementary classroom. *Current Issues in Comparative Education, 5*(1), 7–23.

Bomer, R. (2003). Things that make kids smart: A Vygotskian perspective on concrete tool use in primary literacy classrooms. *Journal of Early Childhood Literacy, 3*(3), 223–247.

Bourdieu, P. (1977). *Outline of a theory of practice.* Cambridge: Cambridge University Press.

Bourdieu, P. (1982/1991). *Language and symbolic power.* Cambridge, MA: Harvard University Press.

Bourdieu, P. (1986). The forms of capital (R. Nice, Trans.). In J. G. Richardson (Ed.), *Handbook of Theory and Research for the Sociology of Education* (pp. 241–258). New York: Greenwood Press.

Bourdieu, P. (1990). *The logic of practice.* Stanford, CA: Stanford University Press.

Bourdieu, P., & Wacquant, L. J. D. (1992). *Invitation to a reflexive sociology.* Chicago: University of Chicago Press.

Brandon, K. (2002, October 20). Kindergarten less playful as pressure to achieve grows. *Chicago Tribune,* p. 1.

Brandt, D., & Clinton, K. (2002). Limits of the local: Expanding perspectives on literacy as a social practice. *Journal of Literacy Research, 34*(3), 337–356.

Bredekamp, S. (1987). *Developmentally appropriate practice in early childhood programs serving children from birth through age 8.* Washington, DC: National Association for the Education of Young Children.

Bredekamp, S., & Copple, C. (Eds.). (1997). *Developmentally appropriate practice in early childhood programs.* Washington, DC: National Association for the Education of Young Children.

Britzman, D. P. (1991). *Practice makes practice: A critical study of learning to teach.* Albany, NY: State University of New York.

Brougère, G. (2006). Toy houses: A socio-anthropological approach to analysing objects. *Visual Communication, 5*(1), 5–24.

Brown, B. (1998). How to do things with things (A toy story). *Critical Inquiry, 24*(4), 935–964.

Buckingham, D. (1997). Dissin' Disney: Critical perspectives on children's media culture. *Media, Culture & Society, 19,* 285–293.

Burman, E. (1994). *Deconstructing developmental psychology.* London: Routledge.

Butler, J. (1990). *Gender trouble: Feminism and the subversion of identity.* New York: Routledge.

Cannella, G. S. (1997). *Deconstructing early childhood education: Social justice and revolution.* New York: Peter Lang.

Cannella, G. S. (2000). Critical and feminist reconstructions of early childhood education: Continuing the conversations. *Contemporary Issues in Early Childhood, 1*(2), 215–221.

Carrington, V. (2003). "I'm in a bad mood. Let's go shopping": Interactive dolls, consumer culture and a "glocalized" model of literacy. *Journal of Early Childhood Literacy, 3*(1), 83–98.

Carrington, V. (2005). New textual landscapes, information, and early literacy. In J. Marsh (Ed.), *Popular culture, new media and digital literacy in early childhood* (pp. 13–27). New York: RoutledgeFalmer.

Cazden, C. B. (1988). *Classroom discourse: The language of teaching and learning.* Portsmouth, NH: Heinemann.

Christian, B., & Bloome, D. (2004). Learning to read is who you are. *Reading and Writing Quarterly, 20*(4), 365–384.

Clay, M. (1993). *An observation survey of early literacy achievement.* Auckland, NZ: Heinemann.

Comber, B. (2003). Critical literacy: What does it look like in the early years? In N. Hall, J. Marsh, & J. Larson (Eds.), *Handbook of early childhood literacy* (pp. 355–368). London: Sage.

Comber, B., & Nichols, S. (2004). Getting the big picture: Regulating knowledge in early childhood literacy curriculum. *Journal of Early Childhood Literacy, 4*(1), 43–63.

Compton-Lilly, C. (2005). "Sounding out": A pervasive cultural model of reading. *Language Arts, 82*(6), 441–451.

Connell, R. W., & Messerschmidt, J. W. (2005). Hegemonic masculinity: Rethinking the concept. *Gender & Society, 19*(6), 829–859.

Connolly, P. (2004). *Boys and schooling in the early years.* London: RoutledgeFalmer.

Corsaro, W. A. (2003). *We're friends right? Inside kids' culture.* Washington, DC: Joseph Henry Press.

Corsaro, W. A., & Eder, D. (1990). Children's peer cultures. *Annual Review of Sociology, 16*, 197–220.

Crawford, G. (2004). *Consuming sport: Fans, sport and culture.* New York: Routledge.

Daniel, R. (2007, March 3). Playing to the test? *Iowa City Press Citizen*, p. 1.

Davies, B. (2003). *Frogs and snails and feminist tales. Preschool children and gender* (Rev. ed.). Cresskill, NJ: Hampton Press.

Davies, B., & Saltmarsh, S. (2007). Gender economies: Literacy and the gendered production of neo-liberal subjectivities. *Gender and Education, 19*(1), 1–20.

de Certeau, M. (1984). *The practice of everyday life* (S. Rendall, Trans.). Berkeley, CA: University of California Press.

Deuze, M. (2009). Media industries, work and life. *European Journal of Communication, 24*(4), 467–480.

Disney Consumer Products. (2010). Disney Princess. Retrieved December 10, 2010, from https://www.disneyconsumerproducts.com/Home/display.jsp?contentId=dcp_home_ourfranchises_disney_princess_us&forPrint=false&language=en&preview=false&imageShow=0&pressRoom=US&translationOf=nul&region=0

do Rozario, R.-A. C. (2004). The princess and the Magic Kingdom: Beyond nostalgia, the function of the Disney Princess. *Women's Studies in Communication, 27*(1), 34–59.

Duckworth, E. (1996). *"The having of wonderful ideas" and other essays on teaching and learning.* New York: Teachers College Press.

Dutro, E. (2002). "Us boys like to read football and boy stuff": Reading masculinities, performing boyhood. *Journal of Literacy Research, 34*(4), 465–500.

Dyson, A. H. (1989). *Multiple worlds of child writers: Friends learning to write.* New York: Teachers College Press.

Dyson, A. H. (1993). From invention to social action in early childhood literacy: A reconceptualization through dialogue about difference. *Early Childhood Research Quarterly, 8*, 409–425.

Dyson, A. H. (1997). *Writing superheroes: Contemporary childhood, popular culture, and classroom literacy.* New York: Teachers College Press.

Dyson, A. H. (2003). *The brothers and sisters learn to write: Popular literacies in childhood and school cultures.* New York: Teachers College Press.

Dyson, A. H. (2006). On saying it right (write): "Fix-its" in the foundations of learning to write. *Research in the Teaching of English, 41*(1), 8–42.

Edmiston, B. W. (2008). *Forming ethical identities in early childhood play.* London: Routledge.

Elgas, P. M., Klein, E., Kantor, R., & Fernie, D. (1988). Play and the peer culture: Play styles and object use. *Journal of Research in Childhood Education, 3*(2), 142–153.

Engeström, Y. (1987). *Learning by expanding: An activity-theoretical approach to developmental research.* Helskinki: Orienta-Konsultit.

Fernie, D. E., Kantor, R., & Madrid, S. (In press). *Weaving a tapestry of daily life in P–16 classrooms: Ethnographic studies of peer cultures and school cultures.* Cresskill, NJ: Hampton Press.

Fernie, D. E., Kantor, R., & Whaley, K. L. (1995). Learning from classroom ethnographies: Same places, different times. In J. A. Hatch (Ed.), *Qualitative research in early childhood settings* (pp. 156–172). Westport, CT: Praeger.

Ferreiro, E., & Teberosky, A. (1982). *Literacy before schooling.* Portsmouth, NH: Heinemann.

Finders, M. J. (1997). *Just girls: Hidden literacies and life in junior high.* New York: Teachers College Press.

Fletcher, R. (2006). *Boy writers: Reclaiming their voices.* Portland, ME: Stenhouse.

Foucault, M. (1972). *The archaeology of knowledge* (A. S. Smith, Trans.). New York: Pantheon.

Foucault, M. (1978). *The history of sexuality: An introduction* (Vol. 1). New York: Random House.

Gee, J. P. (1996). *Social linguistics and literacies: Ideology in Discourses* (2nd ed.). London: RoutledgeFalmer.

Gee, J. P. (1999). *An introduction to discourse analysis: Theory and method.* London: Routledge.

Gee, J. P. (2001). A sociocultural perspective on early literacy development. In D. K. Dickinson & S. B. Neuman (Eds.), *Handbook of early literacy research* (pp. 40–42). New York: Guilford Press.

Gilbert, P. (1992). The story so far: Gender, literacy and social regulation. *Gender and Education, 4*(3), 185–199.

Giroux, H. A. (1997). Are Disney movies good for your kids? In S. R. Steinberg & J. L. Kincheloe (Eds.), *Kinderculture: The corporate construction of childhood* (pp. 53–67). Boulder, CO: Westview Press.

Giroux, H. A. (1999). *The mouse that roared.* Oxford: Rowman & Littlefield.

Goffman, E. (1974). *Frame analysis: An essay on the organization of experience.* New York: Harper & Row.

Goldstein, J., Buckingham, D., & Brougère, G. (2005). *Toys, games and media.* Mahwah, NJ: Lawrence Erlbaum.

Göncü, A. (1993). Development of intersubjectivity in the dyadic play of preschoolers. *Early Childhood Research Quarterly, 8,* 99–116.

Göncü, A. (Ed.). (1999). *Children's engagement in the world: Sociocultural perspectives.* Cambridge, UK: Cambridge University Press.

Goodman, K. S. (1994). Reading, writing, and written texts: A transactional sociopsycholinguistic view. In R. B. Ruddell, M. R. Ruddell & H. Singer (Eds.), *Theoretical models and processes of reading* (4th ed., pp. 1093–1130). Newark, DE: International Reading Association.

Goodman, K. S., Shannon, P., Goodman, Y. M., & Rapoport, R. (Eds.). (2004). *Saving our schools: The case for public education; Saying no to "No Child Left Behind".* Berkeley, CA: RDR Books.

Goldstein, L. S. (2007). Beyond the DAP versus standards dilemma: Examining the unforgiving complexity of kindergarten teaching in the United States. *Early Childhood Research Quarterly, 22*(1), 39–54.

Grieshaber, S., & Cannella, G. S. (Eds.). (2001). *Embracing identities in early childhood education: Diversity and possibilities.* New York: Teachers College Press.

Grumet, M. R. (1988). *Bitter milk: Women and Teaching.* Amherst, MA: University of Massachusetts Press.

Gutiérrez, K. D., & Rogoff, B. (2003). Cultural ways of learning: Individual traits or repertoires of practice. *Educational Researcher, 32*(5), 19–25.

Gutiérrez, K. D., Rymes, B., & Larson, J. (1995). Script, counterscript, and underlife in the classroom: James Brown versus Brown v. Board of Education. *Harvard Educational Review, 65*(3), 445–464.

Haas, L., Bell, E., & Sell, L. (Eds.). (1995). *From mouse to mermaid: The politics of film, gender, and culture.* Bloomington, IN: Indiana University Press.

Hartmann, W., & Brougère, G. (2004). Toy culture in preschool education and children's toy preferences. In J. Goldstein, D. Buckingham, & G. Brougère (Eds.), *Toys, Games, and Media.* Mahwah, NJ: Lawrence Erlbaum.

Hartshorne, C., Weiss, P., & Burks, A. W. (Eds.). (1998). *Collected papers of Charles Sanders Peirce: Elements of logic* (Vol. II). Cambridge, MA: Harvard University Press.

Heath, S. B. (1983). *Ways with words: Language, life, and work in communities and classrooms.* Cambridge: Cambridge University Press.

Hemphill, C. (2006, July 26). In kindergarten playtime, a new meaning for "play" [Electronic version]. *New York Times* Retrieved June 7, 2009, from http://www.nytimes.com/2006/07/26/education/26education.html

Hilton, M. (1996). Manufacturing make-believe: Notes on the toy and media industry for children. In M. Hilton (Ed.), *Potent fictions: Children's literacy and the challenge of popular culture* (pp. 19–46). London: Routledge.

Holdaway, D. (1979). *Foundations of literacy.* Gosford, New South Wales: Ashton Scholastic.

Holland, D., Lachicotte, W., Skinner, D., & Cain, C. (1998). *Identity and agency in cultural worlds.* Cambridge, MA: Harvard University Press.

Iger, B. (2006). Walt Disney Company Annual Meeting of Shareholders 2006. Retrieved December 10, 2010, from http://media.disney.go.com/investor-relations/presentations/060310_transcript.pdf

International Reading Association & National Association for the Education of Young Children. (1998). Learning to read and write: Developmentally appropriate practices for young children. Retrieved December 10, 2010, from www.naeyc.org/files/naeyc/file/positions/PSREAD98.PDF

International Reading Association & National Association for the Education of Young Children. (2009). Where we stand: On learning to read and write. Retrieved April 22, 2011, from http://www.naeyc.org/files/naeyc/file/positions/WWSSLearningToReadAndWriteEnglish.pdf

Ivanič, R. (2004). Discourses of writing and learning to write. *Language and Education, 18*, 220–245.

Jenkins, H. (Ed.). (1998). *The children's culture reader.* New York: New York University Press.

Jenkins, H. (2006). *Convergence culture: Where old and new media collide.* New York: New York University Press.

Jewitt, C. (2006). *Technology, literacy and learning: A multimodal approach.* London: Routledge.

Jewitt, C., & Kress, G. (Eds.). (2003). *Multimodal literacy*. New York: Peter Lang.

Jewitt, C., & Oyama, R. (2001). Visual meaning: A social semiotic approach. In T. van Leeuwen & C. Jewitt (Eds.), *Handbook of Visual Analysis* (pp. 134–156). London: Sage.

Kamler, B. (1994). Gender and genre in early writing. *Linguistics and Education, 6*(2), 153–154.

Kamler, B. (1999). This lovely doll who's come to school: Morning talk as gendered language practice. In B. Kamler (Ed.), *Constructing gender and difference: Critical research perspectives on early childhood* (pp. 191–214). Cresskill, NJ: Hampton Press.

Kanaris, A. (1999). Gendered journeys: Children's writing and the construction of gender, *Language and Education, 13*(4), 254–268.

Kane, D. (2003). Distinction worldwide?: Bourdieu's theory of taste in international context. *Poetics, 31*(5-6), 403–421.

Kantor, R., & Fernie, D. (Eds.). (2003). *Early childhood classroom processes*. Cresskill, NJ: Hampton Press.

Kendrick, M. (2005). Playing house: A "sideways" glance at literacy and identity in early childhood. *Journal of Early Childhood Literacy, 5*(1), 1–28.

Knobel, M., & Lankshear, C. (Eds.). (2007). *The new literacies sampler*. New York: Peter Lang.

Kress, G. (1997). *Before writing: Rethinking the paths to literacy*. London: Routledge.

Kress, G. (2003a). *Literacy in the new media age*. London: Routledge.

Kress, G. (2003b). Perspectives on making meaning: The differential principles and means of adults and children. In N. Hall, J. Larson, & J. Marsh (Eds.), *Handbook of early childhood literacy* (pp. 154–166). London: Sage.

Kress, G. (2009). What is mode? In C. Jewitt (Ed.), *The Routledge handbook of multimodal analysis* (pp. 54–67). London: Sage.

Kress, G., & Jewitt, C. (2003). Introduction. In C. Jewitt & G. Kress (Eds.), *Multimodal literacy* (pp. 1–18). New York: Peter Lang.

Kress, G., & van Leeuwen, T. (1996). *Reading images: The grammar of visual design*. London: Routledge.

Kyratzis, A. (2004). Talk and interaction among children and the co-construction of peer groups and peer culture. *Annual Reviews of Anthropology, 33*, 625–649.

Lacroix, C. (2004). Images of animated others: The orientalization of Disney's cartoon heroines from *The Little Mermaid* to *The Hunchback of Notre Dame*. *Popular Communication, 2*(4), 213–229.

Larson, J. (2002). Packaging process: Consequences of commodified pedagogy on students' participation in literacy events. *Journal of Early Childhood Literacy, 2*(1), 65–94.

Larson, J. (Ed.). (2007). *Literacy as snake oil: Beyond the quick fix* (2nd ed.). New York: Peter Lang.

Lave, J., & Wenger, E. (1991). *Situated learning: Legitimate peripheral participation*. Cambridge: Cambridge University Press.

Leander, K. M. (2002a). Locating Latanya: The situated production of identity artifacts in classroom interaction. *Research in the Teaching of English, 37*(2), 198–250.

Leander, K. M. (2002b). Polycontextual construction zones: Mapping the expansion of schooled space and identity. *Mind, Culture, and Activity, 9*(3), 211–237.

Leander, K. M. (2004). Reading the spatial histories of positioning in a classroom literacy event. In K. M. Leander & M. Sheehy (Eds.), *Spatializing literacy research and practice* (pp. 115–142). New York: Peter Lang.

Lee, L. (2008). Understanding gender through Disney's marriages: A study of young Korean immigrant girls. *Early Childhood Education Journal, 36,* 11–18.

Lensmire, T. (1994). *When children write: Critical re-visions of the writing workshop*. New York: Teachers College Press.

Leont'ev, A. N. (1977). *Activity and consciousness, philosophy in the USSR, problems of dialectical materialism*. Moscow: Progress Publishers.

Lewis, C., Enciso, P., & Moje, E. B. (2007). *Reframing sociocultural research on literacy: Identity, agency, and power*. Mahwah, NJ: Lawrence Erlbaum.

Luke, A. (1992). The body literate: Discourse and inscription in early literacy training. *Linguistics and Education, 4,* 107–129.

Luke, A., Carrington, V., & Kaptitzke, C. (2003). Textbooks and early childhood literacy. In N. Hall, J. Larson, & J. Marsh (Eds.), *Handbook of early childhood literacy* (pp. 249–257). London: Sage.

Luke, A., & Grieshaber, S. (2004). New adventures in the politics of literacy: An introduction. *Journal of Early Childhood Literacy, 4*(1), 5–9.

Luke, C. (1995). Media and cultural studies. In P. Freebody, S. Muspratt, & A. Luke (Eds.), *Constructing critical literacies*. Cresskill, NJ: Hampton Press.

MacGillivray, L., & Martinez, A. M. (1998). Princesses who commit suicide: Primary children writing within and against gender stereotypes. *Journal of Literacy Research, 30,* 53–84.

Magee, M. (2003, July 21). An elementary evolution: Kindergarten literacy push has some teachers worried. *Union-Tribune,* p. 1.

Marsh, J. (2003). Early childhood literacy and popular culture. In N. Hall, J. Larson, & J. Marsh (Eds.), *Handbook of Early Childhood Literacy* (pp. 112–125). London: Sage.

Marsh, J. (2005a). Ritual, performance, and identity construction: Young children's engagement with popular cultural and media texts. In J. Marsh (Ed.), *Popular culture, new media and digital literacy in early childhood* (pp. 28–50). New York: RoutledgeFalmer.

Marsh, J. (Ed.). (2005b). *Popular culture, new media and digital literacy in early childhood*. New York: RoutledgeFalmer.

Marsh, J. (2006). Popular culture in the literacy curriculum: A Bourdieuan analysis. *Reading Research Quarterly, 41*(2), 160–174.

Martens, P. (1996). *I already know how to read: A child's view of literacy*. Portsmouth, NH: Heinemann.

Martin, W., & Dombey, H. (2002). Finding a voice: Language and play in the home corner. *Language and education, 16*(1), 48–61.

Martino, W. (2004). "The boy problem": Boys, schooling, and masculinity. In R. P. Transit (Ed.), *Disciplining the child via the discourse of the professions* (pp. 19–33). Springfield, IL: Charles C. Thomas.

McIntyre, E. (1995). The struggle for developmentally appropriate literacy instruction. *Journal of Research in Childhood Education, 9*(2), 145–156.

Mehan, H. (1979). *Learning lessons: Social organization in the classroom*. Cambridge, MA: Harvard University Press.

Millard, E. (2003). Gender and early childhood literacy. In N. Hall, J. Larson, & J. Marsh (Eds.), *Handbook of Early Childhood Literacy* (pp. 22–33). London: Sage.

Neuman, S. B., & Roskos, K. A. (2005). Whatever happened to developmentally appropriate practice in early literacy? *Beyond the Journal: Young Children on the Web, 60*(4), 1–6. Retrieved December 10, 2010, from http://journal.naeyc.org/btj/200507/02Neuman.pdf

New London Group. (1996). A pedagogy of multiliteracies: Designing social futures. *Harvard Educational Review, 66*, 60–93.

Newkirk, T. (1989). *More than stories: The range in children's writing*. Portsmouth, NH: Heinemann.

Newkirk, T. (2002). *Misreading masculinity: Boys, literacy, and popular culture*. Portsmouth, NH: Heinemann.

Newkirk, T. (2006). Media and literacy: What's good? *Educational Leadership, 64*(1), 62–66.

Newkirk, T. (2007). Popular culture and writing development. *Language Arts, 84*(6), 539–548.

Newkirk, T., & McClure, P. (1992). *Listening in: Children talk about books (and other things)*. Portsmouth, NH: Heinemann.

Nichols, S. (2002). Parents' construction of their children as gendered, literate subjects: A critical discourse analysis. *Journal of Early Childhood Literacy, 2*(2), 123–144.

NCLB. (2002). No child left behind: Closing the achievement gap in America's public schools. Retrieved December 10, 2010, from http://www2.ed.gov/nclb/accountability/achieve/edpicks.jhtml?src=ln

Noon, C. (2005). Iger's Disney Courts Princesses In Huge Campaign. Retrieved December 10, 2010, from http://www.forbes.com/2005/10/03/disney-princesses-dvds-cx_cn_1003autofacescan04.html

Norris, S. (2004). *Analyzing multimodal interaction: A methodological framework*. London: Routledge.

Norris, S. (2006). Multiparty interaction: A multimodal perspective on relevance. *Discourse Studies, 8*(3), 401–421.

Ohanian, S. (2002). *What happened to recess and why are our children struggling in kindergarten?* New York: McGraw-Hill.

Olfman, S. (Ed.). (2003). *All work and no play: How educational reforms are harming our preschoolers*. Westport, CT: Praeger.

Owocki, G. (1995). *Teacher facilitation of play and emergent literacy in preschool*. Unpublished doctoral dissertation, University of Arizona, Tucson, AZ.

Owocki, G. (1999). *Literacy through play*. Portsmouth, NH: Heinemann.

Owocki, G., & Goodman, Y. M. (2002). *Kidwatching: Documenting children's literacy development*. Portsmouth, NH: Heinemann.

Pahl, K., & Rowsell, J. (2010). *Artifactual literacies: Every object tells a story*. New York: Teachers College Press.

Parkes, B., & Smith, J. (1987). *The three little pigs*. Crystal Lake, IL: Rigby.

Pellegrini, A. D., & Galda, L. (1993). Ten years after: A reexamination of symbolic play and literacy research. *Reading Research Quarterly, 28*, 162–175.

Pompe, C. (1996). "But they're pink!"—"Who cares!": Popular culture in the primary years. In M. Hilton (Ed.), *Potent fictions: Children's literacy and the challenge of popular culture* (pp. 92–125). London: Routledge.

Pugh, A. J. (2009). *Longing and belonging: Parents, children, and consumer culture*. Berkeley, CA: University of California Press.

Ranker, J. (2006). "There's fire magic, electric magic, ice magic, or poison magic": The world of video games and Adrian's compositions about Gauntlet Legends. *Language Arts, 84*(1), 21–33.

Ravitch, D. (2010). *The death and life of the great American school system*. New York: Basic Books.

Reid, J. (1999). Little women/little men: Gender, violence, and embodiment in an early childhood classroom. In B. Kamler (Ed.), *Constructing gender and difference: Critical research perspectives on early childhood education* (pp. 167–189). Cresskill, NJ: Hampton Press.

Rogers, R. (Ed.). (2011). *An introduction to critical discourse analysis in education* (2nd ed.). Mahwah, NJ: Lawrence Erlbaum.

Rogoff, B. (1995). Observing sociocultural activity on three planes: Participatory appropriation, guided participation, and apprenticeship. In J. V. Wertsch, P. del Rio, & A. Alvarez (Eds.), *Sociocultural studies of mind* (pp. 139–164). Boston, MA: Cambridge University Press.

Rosenblatt, L. (1978). *The reader, the text, and the poem*. Carbondale, IL: Southern Illinois University.

Roskos, K. A., & Christie, J. F. (2001). Examining the play-literacy interface: A critical review and future directions. *Journal of Early Childhood Literacy, 1*(1), 59–89.

Rousseau, J.-J. (1762/1979). *Emile or on education.* New York: Basic Books.

Rowe, D. W. (1998). The literate potentials of book-related dramatic play. *Reading Research Quarterly, 33*(1), 10–35.

Rowe, D. W. (2000). Bringing books to life: The role of book-related dramatic play in young children's literacy learning. In K. A. Roskos & J. F. Christie (Eds.), *Play and literacy in early childhood: Research from multiple perspectives* (pp. 3–25). Mahwah, NJ: Lawrence Erlbaum Associates.

Rowe, D. W. (2008). Social contracts for writing: Negotiating shared understandings about text in the preschool years. *Reading Research Quarterly, 43*(1), 66–95.

Rowe, D. W. (2010). Directions for studying early literacy as social practice. *Language Arts, 88*(2), 134–143.

Rowsell, J., & Pahl, K. (2007). Sedimented identities in texts: Instances of practice. *Reading Research Quarterly, 42*(3), 388–404.

Sawyer, R. K. (1997). *Pretend play as improvisation: Conversation in the preschool classroom.* Norwood, NJ: Erlbaum.

Sawyer, R. K. (2003). Levels of analysis in pretend play discourse: Metacommunication in conversational routines. In D. E. Lytle (Ed.), *Play and educational theory and practice* (pp. 137–157). Westport, CT: Praeger.

Sax, L. (2007). *Boys adrift: The five factors driving the growing epidemic of unmotivated boys and underachieving young men.* New York: Basic Books.

Schmidt, R. R. (2005). *Broken trust: Teachers' talk about literacy practices in times of federal mandates.* Unpublished doctoral dissertation, University of Iowa, Iowa City.

Scollon, R. (2001a). Action and text: Toward an integrated understanding of the place of text in social (inter)action, mediated discourse analysis and the problem of social action. In R. Wodak & M. Meyer (Eds.), *Methods in critical discourse analysis* (pp. 139–183). London: Sage.

Scollon, R. (2001b). *Mediated discourse: The nexus of practice.* London: Routledge.

Scollon, R., & Scollon, S. W. (2003). *Discourses in place.* New York: Routledge.

Scollon, R., & Scollon, S. W. (2004). *Nexus analysis: Discourse and the emerging internet.* New York: Routledge.

Seiter, E. (1993). *Sold separately: Children and parents in consumer culture.* Piscataway, NJ: Rutgers University Press.

Siegel, M. (2006). Rereading the signs: Multimodal transformations in the field of literacy research. *Language Arts, 84*(1), 65–77.

Siegel, M., Kontovourki, S., Schmier, S., & Enriquez, G. (2008). Literacy in motion: A case study of a shape-shifting kindergartener. *Language Arts, 86*(2), 89–98.

Smith, M. W., & Wilhelm, J. D. (2002). *"Reading don't fix no Chevys": Literacy in the lives of young men.* Portsmouth, ME: Heinemann.

Smith, P. K. (1988). Children's play and its role in early development: A reevaluation of the "Play Ethos". In A. D. Pellegrini (Ed.), *Psychological bases for early education* (pp. 207–226). Chichester, UK: Wiley.

Solsken, J. W. (1993). *Literacy, gender, and work in families and in school.* Norwood, NJ: Ablex.

Stewart, T. L. (2005, November 4). For kindergartners, playtime is over: Full-day schedules, emphasis on learning create "new 1st grade." *Dallas Morning News,* p. 6B.

Stipek, D. (2005). Early childhood education at a crossroads. *Harvard Educational Letter, 2005,* [Electronic Journal]. Retrieved December 10, 2010, from http://www.hepg.org/hel/article/288

Stipek, D. (2006). No Child Left Behind comes to preschool. *Elementary School Journal, 106*(5), 455–465.

Street, B. V. (1995). *Social literacies: Critical approaches to literary development.* Singapore: Pearson Education Asia.

Street, B. V., & Street, J. (1991). The schooling of literacy. In D. Barton & R. Ivanic (Eds.), *Writing in the community* (pp. 143–166). London: Sage.

Sumsion, J. (2005). Male teachers in early childhood education: Issues and case study. *Early Childhood Research Quarterly, 20,* 109–123.

Thorne, B. (1993). *Gender play: Girls and boys in school.* New Brunswick, NJ: Rutgers University Press.

Tobin, J. (1995). The irony of self-expression. *American Journal of Education, 103,* 233–258.

Tobin, J. (2000). *"Good guys don't wear hats": Children's talk about the media.* New York: Teachers College Press.

Tobin, J. (Ed.). (2004). *Pikachu's global adventure: The rise and fall of Pokémon.* Durham, NC: Duke University Press.

Tolchinsky, L. (2003). *The cradle of culture: What children know about writing and numbers before being taught.* Mahwah, NJ: Lawrence Erlbaum.

Trawick-Smith, J. (1998). A qualitative analysis of metaplay in the preschool years. *Early Childhood Research Quarterly, 13*(3), 433–452.

Vasquez, V. M. (2004). *Negotiating critical literacies with young children.* Mahwah, NJ: Lawrence Erlbaum.

Vasquez, V. M. (2005). Resistance, power-tricky, and colorless energy: What engagement with everyday popular culture texts can teach us about learning, and literacy. In J. Marsh (Ed.), *Popular culture, new media and digital literacy in early childhood* (pp. 201–218). New York: RoutledgeFalmer.

Vygotsky, L. (1935/1978). *Mind in society* (A. Luria, M. Lopez-Morillas & M. Cole, Trans.). Cambridge, MA: Harvard University Press.

Walkerdine, V. (1984). Some day my prince will come. In A. McRobbie & M. Nava (Eds.), *Gender and generation* (pp. 162–184). London: Macmillan.

Walkerdine, V. (1990). *Schoolgirl fictions.* New York: Verso.

Walkerdine, V. (1994). Femininity as performance. In L. D. Stone & G. M. Boldt (Eds.), *The education feminism reader* (pp. 57–69). London: Routledge.

Weil, E. (2007, June 3). When should a kid start kindergarten? *New York Times Magazine.* Retrieved December 10, 2010, from http://www.nytimes.com/2007/06/03/magazine/03kindergarten-t.html?pagewanted=all

Wells, G. (1986). *The meaning makers: Children learning language and using language to learn.* Portsmouth, NH: Heinemann.

Wertsch, J. V. (1991). *Voices of the mind: A sociocultural approach to mediated action.* Cambridge, MA: Harvard University Press.

Wertsch, J. V., del Rio, P., & Alvarez, A. (1995). Sociocultural studies: History, action, and mediation. In J. V. Wertsch, P. del Rio, & A. Alvarez (Eds.), *Sociocultural studies of mind* (pp. 1–34). Cambridge, UK: Cambridge University Press.

Whannel, G. (2001). *Media sports stars: Masculinities and moralities.* London: Routledge.

Whitmore, K. F., & Goodman, Y. M. (1995). Transforming curriculum in language and literacy. In S. Bredekamp & R. Teresa (Eds.), *Reaching potentials: Transforming early childhood curriculum and assessment* (pp. 145–166). Washington, DC: National Association for the Education of Young Children.

Whitmore, K. F., Goodman, Y. M., Martens, P., & Owocki, G. (2004). Critical lessons from the transactional perspective on early literacy research. *Journal of Early Childhood Literacy, 4*(3), 291–325.

Wohlwend, K. E. (2004). Chasing friendship: Acceptance, rejection, and recess play. *Childhood Education, 81*(2), 77–82.

Wohlwend, K. E. (2007a). Friendship meeting or blocking circle?: Identities in the laminated spaces of a playground conflict *Contemporary Issues in Early Childhood, 8*(1), 73–88.

Wohlwend, K. E. (2007b). *Kindergarten as nexus of practice: A mediated discourse analysis of reading, writing, play, and design practices in an early literacy apprenticeship.* Unpublished doctoral dissertation, University of Iowa, Iowa City.

Wohlwend, K. E. (2008). Play as a literacy of possibilities: Expanding meanings in practices, materials, and spaces. *Language Arts, 86*(2), 127–136.

Wohlwend, K. E. (2009a). Dilemmas and discourses of learning to write: Assessment as a contested site. *Language Arts, 86*(5), 341–351.

Wohlwend, K. E. (2009b). Mediated discourse analysis: Researching children's nonverbal interactions as social practice. *Journal of Early Childhood Research, 7*(3), 228–243.

Index

About the Author

Karen Wohlwend is an assistant professor in literacy, culture, and language education at Indiana University. Her research reconceptualizes play as a literacy for reading and writing identity texts and as a tactic for participating and learning in early childhood classrooms. Wohlwend is the author of numerous articles that provide a critical perspective on children's play and literacies, popular media, gender, and identity. The research in this book was recognized through the 2008 International Reading Association Outstanding Dissertation Award.